About the Author

JO CARROLL decided that thirty years working with traumatised children was long enough. Besides, if she left it much longer she would be too creaky to fulfil her adolescent dream of travelling round the world. So, armed with little more than general ignorance, a diary, and insatiable curiosity, off she went. A grown-up gap year. Except she didn't always feel like a grown-up.

Many of those who joined me on my travels or who supported
me back home can be found in this book. Most appear under
their own names. Other names have been changed – mainly
because I have not been able to contact them to get permission
to include them in my story, or because I felt that some
protection was necessary.

I should also point out that I have two brothers. Their roles
have been amalgamated in this text.

Find me on Twitter at @jomcarroll
On Facebook at
https://www.facebook.com/profile.php?id=739344134

Blogs of this book, and the trip that preceded it:
http://gapyearsthebook.blogspot.com
http://whereivegone.blogspot.com

Cover design by Mark Smart.

JO CARROLL

OVER THE HILL AND FAR AWAY

One Grown-Up Gap Year

If with me you'll fondly stray

Over the hills and far away.

(*The Beggars' Opera*, by John Gay)

OVER THE HILL AND FAR AWAY

CONTENTS

Dislocated in Oz	7
From Cath to Bertha	25
Tika to the Rescue	55
I am a Dreadful Memsahib	89
Defeated by India	123
Waiting in Malaysia	153
Baby Days	171
Balmy Days	175
Not The End of the Story	203
Two Years Later	235
Acknowledgements	239

PART ONE

DISLOCATED IN OZ

1.

I blame *The Guardian*. If they hadn't published an article entitled 'Gap Years are Wasted on the Young' I wouldn't be standing in the scrum of Sydney Airport at 6.30 in the morning, propped on a luggage trolley, surrounded by what feels like two thousand adolescents with muscles and surfboards.

'Suppose they're looking for drugs,' a young man mutters to his friend. They clutch their surfboards, inviting my imagination to fill them with heroin.

To my astonishment a man, wearing a uniform that looks as though he's worn it all night, notices my weariness.

'You got any food with you?' he asks. The tannoy has warned us, over and over, that importing food is a heinous crime.

'No!'

I make no mention of the packet of crisps I had secreted from the plane. He makes no mention of drugs. Surely he can see I am a child of the Sixties, with my unruly hair and rucksack? Maybe he presumes I have more sense these days.

I do have more sense these days. I did my share of inhaling, before adulthood set in, before I took account of health warnings and legal consequences and all the other baggage that comes with the realities of conformity.

He gives me a green pass and hustles me away through the security gates. I totter into the streets of Sydney.

I hope I look as if I know where I'm going. Around me the streets overflow with the young and vigorous, the surfeit of youth serving only to underline my wrinkles and the bags under my eyes. In the park I dodge joggers, some running steadily and checking their watches, others pink and panting and hoping no one will notice if they walk a few paces. A woman with the tottering run of a mother in high heels stops to pull up her red leggings; men shoot baskets; others play football with goalposts marked by jackets and ties; in one corner a group of kick-boxers fight imaginary enemies; in another a gaggle of women contort themselves with the aid of giant elastic bands. It is my first encounter with the determined athletes of Sydney.

I perch on a bench, apparently invisible to all these pink and puffing people. They don't make me feel old, exactly; just unfit. Well, that's what I tell myself. A good enough reason to leave them to their efforts.

As I wander towards the Harbour I stumble across a free didgeridoo concert. I might as well go in, given that I have no other plans for today; or tomorrow. I have missed the first ten minutes, find a seat in the darkened hall and succumb to the compulsive rhythm of the music while lights dance across the backdrop of desert and lonely cacti. The musician, with distinctive brown skin and flattened features, cheeks puffed with blowing his instrument, uses his hands with the skill of a ballet dancer to suggest a kookaburra, a crocodile, a kangaroo. Before each tune he tells its story, related in a sonorous voice that echoes in this near-empty space, tales from his tribe and from his childhood. He inhales (his chest must reach down to his toes it takes so long) and then the didgeridoo begins its booming. My feet are tapping; my shoulders swaying; I am enthralled with the magic of his stories. At the end, I have forgotten every word, retaining little more than an unexpected feeling of elation and the boom of didgeridoo in my ears.

As the lights go up I stumble to the front of the hall with my notebook and ask the performer to write his name and its meanings: Yongurra (descendant of the turtle, soft-bellied and hard-shelled) Yerin (the lost one) Bungarinyi (his family name) Dumtjaa (his clan, from the north of Queensland). Then he asks me my name. It feels as if he is simply being polite. Maybe it's the jetlag that makes me stumble over my reply. While his name embraces his story and that of his tribe mine says nothing about who I am, nor where I have come from. Or even what I am doing here. I have been asking myself the same question for the last twenty-four hours.

2.

It began two years ago, as drizzle brought autumn to an August morning, and I stumbled down to breakfast with all the enthusiasm of Monday. A solitary wine glass, stained vinegary red, stood by the sink. The cat, as usual, caressed my legs until I fed her. A child flapped her fingers along the railings outside my window. I flicked on the radio, crooned along with 'You've Lost That Lovin' Feelin''; I blamed the weather. The kettle boiled. I sat down with my cereal and *The Guardian* and the world changed.

'Gap Years are Wasted on the Young.' The article looked at the difficulties of young British Asians taking time out. It was interesting but soon forgotten. It was the headline that captivated. I reached for the scissors, cut out the precious words, clipped them to a notice board, hid them in a drawer, retrieved them and left them isolated on my table. Bells from adolescent fantasies clanged. Could I? Could I really?

I was fifty-four, living in an ordinary house in an ordinary street in a market town in Wiltshire. Not many people know Wiltshire. Wiltshire smells of sheep in late April, oily sheep with ragged coats that trail behind them in the spring sunshine, lambs with limbs on springs and the plaintive bleat of the lost. The Downs sing with the trill of the skylark, the swoop and play of swallows. From the top of Martinsell Hill the fields are rich with the soft green of new wheat, the vulgar yellow of oil-seed rape. A blue haze hangs over Salisbury Plain; my mind's eye reaches to Stonehenge, the great spire of the Cathedral, and beyond it to the sea.

I slumped in my ordinary kitchen. The window needed painting. The tap dripped and I reminded myself to phone a plumber. No, I can't change a tap-washer myself. Then my gaze crept back to that headline. That Dream – left over from the Sixties – stared back at me. Many of us have Those Dreams: to dance at Covent Garden, to ride a motorbike at Silverstone, to learn to fly. Dreams that grow dormant as the demands of work and family absorb our youthful energies. Mine was to go round the world.

Suddenly, surprising me with the vigour of a forgotten love, I uncovered the fantasies of my youth. What does the jungle smell like? Is it possible to live on nothing but rice? Are the colours in India as vibrant as the photographs suggest they are?

And then, as vivid as my adolescent fantasies, came other memories. My older brother, defying parental opposition and taking himself off in a Land Rover with a friend, returning on Boxing Day, two-and-a-half years later, with an Australian accent and frostbite. Every couple of weeks the postman would knock, wait for my mother to open a flimsy blue airmail letter and confirm where he was, so he could pass the news along the street ensuring that Mr Rose and Mrs Vernon were kept up to date. Every month or so a small box of slides appeared: my brother in Athens, in Ankara, camping on the Khyber Pass.

I wanted to follow him. But I didn't. My father was thin-lipped whenever I floated the idea. I didn't need him to open his mouth to hear his objections.

'Look at you, what do you know about going round the world? Just because you've made it to university, you think you know everything. Besides, you haven't any money. What would you live on?' (The subtext: I'm not going to help with such a hare-brained idea.)

My mother simply cried, her opposition drowned in tears. Her world was unsafe for women; they learned shorthand and typing, married, made tea for their husbands, stopped working when babies came. My going to university was dangerous enough.

Nevertheless, I talked about going. Feasted on my brother's letters, and – once he was home – the tales that never made it as far as my parents.

Looking back, from the comfort of my Wiltshire kitchen, I thought about what really stopped me. Maybe, in spite of my loudmouthing, underneath it all I believed my parents were right. The world was too dangerous for women; and I was too feeble to tackle it alone. Were those excuses that had kept me safely at home all these years a smokescreen for a lack of bottle? Forget the pedantic curiosity of my youth. The real reason I wanted to travel, now, was to see if I could.

Was this really a good enough reason? It surely minimised the significance of my decision to the level of wondering if I could learn to play the saxophone, or grow prize potatoes. But it seemed a good enough reason at the time. And, in my months of travelling, I never found a better one.

I shook myself. I'd be late for work if I wallowed in illusions like this. I clattered round the kitchen, shuffling bowls in the sink; my hands were occupied but my mind was not deceived. I leaned against the warmth of the Rayburn, hoping its solidity would stifle these wild imaginings. I tried to sit with the cat for a while, believing her softness would soothe me, but I approached her with such purpose that she fled through the cat flap with all the urgency of an animal expecting the flea spray.

I retreated to the table. I'd worked for thirty years in child and adolescent mental health; they would manage without me for half an hour. If they could manage for half an hour, then they could manage for twelve months.

But was I ready to manage without them? That was easier to answer. I had spent too long working with child trauma, sitting on the floor with children who could only hurl toys across the room in rage, or who quivered with fear at the prospect of my closing the door. Children who spat at me, hurled cups of coffee at me, practised every term of abuse at me. Many of whom, after months and sometimes years of gentle playing, could laugh at last and no longer needed me.

I had lived with the tales of the worst that men and women can do to children; and it no longer surprised me. I had lost the urge to vomit at each new tale of abuse. I wondered if I still understood shocking. Without that sense of horror, I was already beginning to question how much longer I could be effective in a job I had loved for all those years.

Easy, of course, to be disillusioned with any job after thirty years. But it had been my career. People knew who I was. I spoke at conferences. Occasionally people would come up to me and say, 'so you're Jo Carroll.' As if the few articles and one book that I'd written made me different. They were moments of recognition, of achievement. Could I manage if nobody knew who I was?

Could I manage without my daughters? All adult now, coming and going as adult daughters do. They did not have the childhoods I would have chosen for them; divorce, remarriage, widowhood: bald facts that would suggest a misery memoir though we didn't see it like that. We were simply dealing with the cards that life dealt us, like any other family. Only the youngest was still at university. It was reasonable – surely – to assume that soon they would all be on their way. I reached for a pen and paper and wrote:

Reasons to go round the world:
I want to.
I've always wanted to (I think).
Reasons why I should go round the world now:
My daughters will soon have graduated and be launched into their own lives.
It is likely to be a while before grandchildren tug at my sleeves (I got that one wrong!).
I want to go while I still have working knees.
Reasons why I shouldn't go round the world:
??

I stared in disbelief. Could it really be that easy? As I sit sipping coke in Sydney Harbour, boats chugging in front of me and the glorious wings of the Opera House pink in the evening light, I can't quite believe I took such a huge decision in a few minutes on the basis of scribbled notes on the back of an envelope.

Of course, I lost count of second thoughts. Questions sang in the quiet night moments. Cuddled under my duvet, disturbed by the hoot of an owl, my stomach ached with foreboding. What if I got lost, ill, mugged? I forced myself to keep this list short. I'd never done anything like this before; group holidays had built-in safety procedures; this would be proper travelling and I didn't know the rules. What if my daughters were lost, ill, mugged – needed their mother? Would anyone notice if I simply checked into a hotel at Heathrow Airport and wrote a blog from there, culled from internet searches, a collection of *Lonely Planets* and a thorough reading of Bill Bryson?

I made myself tell people. The more people knew, I reasoned, the harder it would be to back down.

'How brave,' some said.

'No,' I replied: 'it would be so much worse to turn round when I'm eighty and wish I'd gone.'

Who was I trying to convince?

More significantly, could I convince my daughters? I told Anna, the eldest, first.

'How will you manage without libraries?' she asked. She knows me too well.

'I'm sure I'll find books,' I said, as if I knew. 'Besides, I'm beginning in Australia and New Zealand – it'll be easy there. I'll have got the hang of the book-thing by the time I get to Nepal and India.' She raised her eyebrows in a who-are-you-kidding way, and said nothing.

Next, I told Tessa.

'Be careful,' she began. Then stopped. She lived in Caracas; I did not need to remind her of her broken promise not to visit Bogotá. Following which she admitted that Caracas is the more dangerous city, as if that might make me feel better. 'Just look after yourself.' (But she does understand travelling. In five months' time she will send me new knickers for my birthday, recognising that the few I'd taken with me would be disintegrating.)

Annie, the eldest stepdaughter, announced that she was not surprised. How could she not be surprised, when I surprised myself? She shrugged, hugged me.

'You were never going to retire in the corner with your knitting, were you?' she said. My venture felt a rather extreme alternative to knitting.

Polly was emerging from the chrysalis of being the youngest. She thought for a while, then asked about flights and itineraries and hotels. She introduced me to quad-band phones, internet cafés, and made me practise text messaging. She followed her first degree with a Masters, and, just before I left, I realised I would be away for her graduation. She told me that it didn't matter, but we both knew it did.

Two weeks before I left they organised a surprise party, which I almost missed. I spent Saturday morning at the market, joshing with the vendors on the fruit and veg stall, stopping in a café to read the local paper, deciding I wouldn't miss the never-ending dispute about parking charges. I was wandering home when my phone rang.

'I'm at The Bear,' Anna said, 'come and join me.'

'I can't. I'm meeting Tessa at the Roebuck later.'

'It's fine. I'll phone Tessa – we'll all meet up here.'

'No, honestly – she'll be waiting for me. I'll meet up with her and come back to you.'

'Just a minute.' I could hear muffled chattering, which I later learned went along the lines of, 'bloody hell, if she can't even get to a surprise party without a performance, how is she going to manage on the other side of the world?'

And then Tessa came on the phone. 'Mum, Anna rang me earlier. I was going to ring you – so it's fine; we'll meet here.' I arrived to find friends and decorations and wine and buckets of good wishes. Any reservations they may have had about my trip kept firmly in the cellar. We dispersed after a couple of hours, and I helped myself to a handful of tinsel.

'I shall tie this to my rucksack,' I said. 'That's how I'll know it's mine. Each time I pick it up, I'll think of you.'

They scattered to their own homes and I was left with the biggest question of all: how would I manage on my own? Time might have changed since the late Sixties; email has replaced airmail letters; phone calls don't need to be booked in advance from crackly offices any more. But I would still have to face the reality of solitude. I'd grown used to it at home, living on my own since my husband died and learning to enjoy the liberties that come with independent living: eating, sleeping, reading, using the bathroom without taking anyone else's needs into account. There are friends around the corner, on the telephone, should I wish for company.

But where would I find those conversations, trivial to the observer, that help to make sense of experiences, shape ideas, and generally keep emotions under control? My richest companion would have to be my diary. It would contain the claptrap of my thinking, never complain about repetition, hesitation, deviation, nor answer back. It would be my comfort blanket, my transitional object. But it could not tap me on the shoulder and suggest I think twice, only provide the dumping ground for mistakes after I had made them. I knew that there would be times when I would wake in an unknown bed in a room smelling of mould and my mouth thick with sleep, and feel forgotten. And that I would wander to breakfast and swallow envy at the sight of families chatting around me. New experiences would tumble through my mind and remain unwashed by the succour of discussion.

I sip my coke, flat by now. I've come this far just to see if I could. I have a year of travelling ahead of me, with only the vaguest idea where I might go. Hardly surprising that the Aboriginal with the wonderful name raised his eyebrows.

3.

As I promised Anna, I am beginning somewhere predictable, where English is spoken and I can understand train timetables. I can practise packing and unpacking, sleeping in hostel dormitories with young people who snore, finding cheap restaurants, lugging my rucksack – still wearing its full complement of tinsel from my leaving party.

Since I've come this far, I might as well do what tourists do in Sydney. I join the swarm heading for Manly, a beach frequented by Sydney's young and beautiful. We saunter, the crowds and I, along a street lined with shops rich with fish and chips, t-shirts, and plastic balls. No one takes any notice of me – well, they wouldn't, would they? Wrinklies have little to contribute in their beautiful world.

I find a shady corner, my back against the sea wall, where I can savour the rumble of the sea, the tang of salt in the air, the occasional screech of gulls, and resist the urge to smile at the healthy bodies around me. The women are tossing hair and wobbling cleavages, men rippling their muscles, trying not to cough on cigarettes and littering sentences with 'fucks' in their efforts to impress. The group closest to me eventually move away to the 'fucking water slides', leaving their sizeable territory marked by empty drinks cartons. An unclaimed beach ball drifts along the sand. Two men wrestle in the breaking waves.

Meanwhile, I am wrapped in the invisibility of middle-aged women, free to observe, to scribble in my diary, without the risk that anyone will peer over my shoulder. Eventually even this palls. Observation becomes tedious; I need to do something or I risk feeling sorry for myself. I dare not face self-pity this early in the trip.

I had earlier rejected the idea of a ten-kilometre walk; this was to be a rest day. But, with no one to keep an eye on my clothes, swimming is not an option. I consult my map and head off across the headland. It's not so far, I reason, to walk inland on roads and return along the cliff path. I love walking, am used to striding across the Wiltshire Downs; a stroll is just what I need. I linger to marvel at the shock of bougainvillea, breath jasmine and frangipani spilling across pathways and imagine myself in a novel by Peter Carey, take photographs of scarlet bottlebrush blossoms stark against the blue Australian sky.

I drop down into Spit, to find the noticeboard at the start of the walk. It will take me three to four hours, it tells me, to return to the beach at Manly. Such predictions are usually generous, but I wonder what time it gets dark here, and if the twilight lingers as it does at home. It is already a quarter to five, but the sun seems high enough in the sky. I consult the map again; it is divided neatly into timed stretches and possible retreats to a road, and so I stride off unperturbed. Well, as unperturbed as anyone can be, wandering along cliff tops and through woodland with nothing but a map and optimism.

It is an easy walk to the first cove, where families are collecting picnic debris and urging children into cars. I reach an inlet, sand gritty in my walking sandals, then ford a burbling stream and clamber back up to a clearer path leading into woodland. The sun is lower, stretching orange fingers across the sea. I try to convince myself that I am not worried, though I am concerned enough to ask a tanned jogger with unusually hairy legs (his shorts are very short) when it will get dark.

'You've half an hour, darling, till the sun goes down, and about another half an hour of twilight, then it will be pitch black. You won't make it to Manly; you might make it to Forty Baskets (three kilometres away), if you hurry. You can catch a bus from there. But you'd be best to turn back to a road, darling.' He does not actively try to stop me as I head for Forty Baskets; I must look as if I know what I'm doing.

The first unnecessary detour takes me towards a rocky outcrop, rewarded with a view of boats bobbing peacefully in the bay and a close encounter with a bright red parrot which allows me to take three photographs before being disturbed by the flash and flying off.

The second detour takes me down a narrow path, common sense deserting me as I slither down rocks, following what appears to be a defined path, sliding on my bottom and dropping onto the sand below. By the time I am convinced I am in the wrong place the sun is well over the horizon and I am on a beach staring up at a cliff face with no idea how to climb back up. The sea, stained pink by the setting sun, is creeping about five centimetres higher with each wave.

I flop on the sand; I've been away for three days and already I am lost. I refuse to think about tales of the notoriously poisonous snakes and spiders of Australia. I will not notice my clammy hands nor thumping heart; my body is clearly anxious but there is no need for my mind to join in. I will not remind myself that it was my silly idea to walk here, to visit Australia, to come travelling in the first place. No, I must work out a solution. If I cannot find a way off the beach in the gloom I can creep into a high-enough corner (I hope) and wait until morning. I shall phone the hostel, tell them where I am (I do not check if there is a signal on my phone as I cannot bear it if there is none). The rocks look bigger, darker, more threatening every time I look at them. The sea transforms from a romantic evening purple to ghostly grey. This might be an adventure to the young still strutting their stuff on the beach at Manly. To me, it feels stomach-churning – I refuse to use the word frightening; I will keep big words like that for another day.

I walk the length of the beach – and find footprints. They are longer than mine; someone else has been here, and isn't here now. A Man Friday solution: I follow them to the cliff face, about three metres high, where they seem to disappear. Close scrutiny reveals strategic hand- and foot-holds; it seems I have no alternative but to climb. It is a climb designed for the long-limbed, not a woman in her mid-fifties with knees that remind her when it's winter. But necessity and adrenalin drives me up it, back into the woodland where I had met the 'darling' man. I dare not sink on a sandy corner in relief; I can only gallop through the almost-dark, past the signpost I had missed on my way, and head to the safety of a car park. A kookaburra laughs as darkness falls like ink and I reach the reprieve of tarmac. I head off in a hopeful direction; there is yet more stumbling along ill-lit roads before I catch the right bus and finally alight at Manly.

I am urgently thirsty. I hobble to the nearest café: first water, then wine, then fish and chips. And time to reflect.

What a twit! I have alarmed myself more than necessary. I've escaped with nothing worse than a blister, and have the decency to feel a little foolish; this trip is not about taking stupid risks. I flounder through an internal dialogue, fine-tuning a serious telling-off and – at the same time – congratulating myself that I have emerged unscathed.

I am reluctant to use the word adventure: it speaks of swashbuckling and trekking through deserts on donkeys. I left home wondering if I had the courage to do this. There were times, on that beach, when I was convinced I couldn't.

Even now, fortified with food and wine and stern self-talking, the prospect of tottering round the world alone looks absurd. No more ridiculous risk-taking, I tell myself. Then grin. Even I know I'm unlikely to listen to advice like that.

4.

It is time to write my first blog home. Unlike my brother, confined to precious letters, I have instant contact with friends and family – text messages on my mobile phone, and the blog. Do I confess to getting lost within days of my arrival? My mother used to scan my brother's letters for his 'between-the-lines' news. He told me, afterwards, of excitements in Kathmandu and Bangkok, young-man adventures that never reached the ears of my parents.

I have no doubt that my daughters conspire behind my back, but to my face they have given me nothing but encouragement. Admitting foolishness this early in the trip feels an unnecessary addition to whatever fantasies they are already entertaining about my travels. I feel a need to reward them with tales of evenings at the Opera House and the glories of museums. I relegate my Manly detour to a joke at the end of the blog; already I am dissembling. But my brother will ask knowing questions when I get home.

I retreat, shamefaced, into the bosom of distant family in Inverell, Northern New South Wales. I haven't seen them for over forty years. I have abandoned one family at home, only to turn to another as soon as I falter at the first hurdle. Feeble? Of course.

But they, too, don't need to know about Manly. Besides, I am looking forward to seeing them.

Bruce's heavy frame is instantly recognisable as I totter from the train. He seizes my rucksack as he would a sack of fertilizer, and I scramble to keep up with him as he heads for the car. The journey to their farm is filled with family news;

who is now married, has died, had more children. I am flooded with names of relations; without the benefit of a family tree I have no idea how they all fit together. But I am absorbed, instantly, into the mayhem, the intrigues, the arguments, the sheer fun of family life.

Their lives, like mine, are changing. While many members of this large extended family live close by, their offspring are not interested in continuing to work the family farm. New agricultural methods and the impact of international markets have changed the face of farming across the world; young people are lured by city lights. My daughters' dreams are not so different.

Age limits Bruce's energy now; he has recently let his land to a tenant. Yet he still charges across the farm like an old bull. He is a solid, heavy man, sagging around the middle, with the eyes of an eagle and the grizzly voice of an Australian Johnny Cash. He invites me to join him, on the back of his quad bike, as he hurtles around the farm.

We ignore the 'no passengers' notice clamped to the bike, and the dusty helmets on a rusty hook in the shed by the back door. (What was that I said about risk-taking?) We bound out of the yard with childish enthusiasm; the wind sweeps my hair and I cling on with the delusion of youth. Our first stop: a huge wooden shed. Bruce wanders across with lead in his steps. At first glance it is just a creaky wooden structure, with crumbling corners, forgotten, idle, silent. It is the old shearing shed.

'We had two thousand sheep here.' Bruce is almost talking to himself. 'Guy who leases the farm now decided they weren't worth the effort, got rid of them.' We climb the few steps into the shed; smells of sheep and wool and machines still linger. I am shown the narrow channels where animals would be hassled to waiting shearers, their clippers attached to an overhead power cable. Bruce grabs a set of rusty shears, flicks a switch and the system lurches into action, the surprised roar of the motor echoing off the empty wooden walls.

'We got through about a hundred sheep a day.' He pauses, wheezes. 'Not like now; modern sheds can manage a hundred and fifty.' He looks smaller in here, diminished.

'And the fleeces would be brought over here.' He waves to an empty space, once the site of a huge table. 'They used to clip the edges, sort for quality, then chuck them in the bins.'

His hand strokes the edge of a polished shelf; he stares across the emptiness as if his ears still hear the bleating of the sheep, the roar of machines, the ripe language of the shearers. He shrugs eventually, and we return to the bike.

I turn, for a last look at this sad shed. He must see it every day. Age and market forces have forced him into unwilling retirement while his land lives on without him. I gave back my office keys and my swipe card, abandoned my professional memberships, and turned my back on work that had been as fulfilling as Bruce's in its way – only one month ago.

Surely it was longer than that? Shouldn't I be grieving? Colleagues keep in touch by email, but confidential details that used to absorb me are carefully excluded and our correspondence is little more than gossip. What might have happened to … I trawl through names of children I worked with. Some are living, safely, with foster parents. Others are less safely held by a system that struggles to understand their behaviour. The face of one little girl flashes in front of me; the details of her infancy are sickening but her foster mother loves her; only time will tell if the work that we have all done will be enough for her to sustain any joy in her childhood.

I will not be there to see it. And, I realise, with a teaspoonful of guilt, I don't miss her. She is safe, and loved.

The process of leaving was a challenge, of course. I had contracts to complete, children I couldn't let down. It took two years, from deciding to embark on this trip until my leaving do. Some colleagues were openly envious; that was easy to deal with. Others more subtly, destructively, so, with side-comments about people who had the money to go swanning off while they had to think about their pensions. Many used the term 'brave'; I now see that it was a substitute for 'reckless'. A word so appropriate now, given that I have already retreated into the safety net of family. Surely I won't spend my year lurching from one landing stage to another?

I follow Bruce back to the quad bike, ignore the creak of my knees as I scramble astride it. (I had minor knee surgery four years ago; already they are protesting at having to carry a heavy rucksack. I tell them to be quiet.) We bounce off around the farm, inspecting gates and water troughs. The land is withered and brown. Months of drought have left farmers throughout New South Wales struggling to keep their animals healthy.

We trundle up a rutted track to stop beside a clump of meagre trees; twigs and branches are scattered across the ground like old bones. Bruce slumps against a tree trunk and waves across the acres in front of us.

'This is – was – all ours.'

I look away; there is a break in his voice and I am sure he would not wish me to see him weep. We were both brought up to believe that men don't cry. Brown fields stretch as far as we can see. Some are dotted with cows, too far away for their emaciation to be visible from here. Others have hints of crops, virgin shoots that should grow into wheat and barley and oats, but are likely to shrivel in these months of drought. Most are simply scrubby.

Bruce turns away; I can find nothing comforting to say to him. So we can only bound off again around the farm. My sheer enjoyment of riding the quad bike fits incongruously with his melancholy, but he grins when I shriek my delight as we career around corners and over ridges; I am obviously forgiven.

Then we come across a blocked water trough. Bruce rolls up his sleeves and releases a ballcock, allowing a whoosh of water to rush into the tank, already heavy with mud and silt. I join in, sinking my arm into stinking water, lifting handfuls of muck from the bottom of the tank and flinging it to the ground (and yes, all over my trousers). We are both, briefly, useful.

PART TWO

FROM CATH TO BERTHA

5.

I do not have a peaceful week with the family, but it is fun. I am introduced to the entire population of Inverell. I drool over a new baby, sit up late at barbecues talking of their children, my children. It feels like a holiday. But somehow I have to gather myself, my stomach-full of nerves, my rucksack still sporting its complement of tinsel, and head off.

Besides, I have agreed to meet Cath in Brisbane. She is a wiry, eagle-eyed Scotswoman. Nobody believes she is seventy-five.

Before I left home I sat with numerous friends, rehearsing my reasons for travelling.

'It's not that I need to be alone,' I explained, 'simply that I want to see the world. Anyone is welcome to join me along the way.' Cath is the mother of a friend. She lives in Brighton, but has spent the last month with Australian relatives. I have met her only once before, but love her daughter and trust her judgment that we will rub along together.

Cath stands in the doorway of our hotel room, a wiry woman bent under a giant blue rucksack, waving a book of Australian poetry that she has found in a second-hand bookshop. Suddenly the room smells of old paper and Cath is quoting a poem that I instantly forget. She abandons her luggage like litter, and we race off to explore Brisbane. Her energy is formidable. She makes me feel old.

It is odd, being with a mother, even one that is not related to me. Mine died in her early seventies, shortly before my husband. She had been ill for several years; her enthusiasm was undimmed but her breathing could not keep up with it. I am out of practice at being with a mother. I'm not sure if I should be looking after her. I ought, at least, to appear capable.

Cath strides, defying her years. I scuttle behind her. She pauses to admire a mighty jacaranda tree dropping a carpet of blue petals over the grey street with the enthusiasm of a child discovering spring.

'Right,' she says, 'I'm going to find the Cathedral.' With that she marches off in the wrong direction. I scamper after her, pointing to the map.

'Good to know,' she says. It will become her catchphrase. Together we head into the city.

'Useless with maps,' she says, as if this is something she is proud of. 'And I can forget anything. Left the baby in the garden once, when we were going out. Filled the car up to take the others to school, and one of them noticed that the baby was missing. Still, no harm done.' So this is what it is like, being with a mother. How will we manage in the enormity of Australia? Are we seriously going to share a campervan in New Zealand? (Is this how my daughters felt when I strode off into the wilderness?)

I have misjudged her. Yes, she loses keys, glasses, purse and herself. But she quotes Christina Rossetti when she climbs hills; Gerard Manley Hopkins when we are stuck in a swamp; Robbie Burns when we are serenaded by a blackbird. I bridle when, during our visit to a gold mine, a wrinkled miner responds to the music of her voice with 'Jesus Bloody Christ' in a mock Scottish accent. Cath is unperturbed. As we turn to leave she stands in the centre of the pathway with her hands on her hips and sings: 'We're no' awa' tae bide awa.' My friend – her daughter – would be proud of her.

Her daughter – my friend – would she be as proud of me? Our friendship began at work, when our children were little and my husband was alive. In time I asked her to supervise my clinical practice; those sessions over we used to linger over cups of tea and talk about our children, our mothers. The conversations that kept us going as women. In time we talked about this trip.

She is one of a little army of women at home. One is answering all my post. Several foster my plants. A third distributes the blog to those without email. I wouldn't be here without them. Not because I need their permission, but because they are my launch pad and my landing ground. The world is scary enough as it is; it would be terrifying without them.

Cath punctures my dreaming. She has decided she needs to visit the museum. She has got lost twice this morning. This time I shall go with her. (I will not tell her about Manly.)

6.

Cath seems to think that I know what I'm doing. I cannot disabuse her. It is my idea to take the train to Cairns. I have environmental pretensions, and hope to minimise the impact of my travelling indulgences. Well, that's my excuse. Environmental guilt is probably a more accurate term. I cannot escape the fact that wandering around the world is not an ideal use of its resources. But I will pay lip service to restricting my profligacy. I find train times, and phone a campsite in Cairns to book a cabin.

'Good to know,' Cath says.

We settle in a tiny carriage which smells of yesterday's sweat. We are armed with plenty of bread and wine; they provide ample distraction from the discomfort of our compartment. I find my game of travel Scrabble.

'Do you want to score?' I ask.

'Do you really care who wins?'

'Couldn't give a toss.'

'Good to know.' We settle with our tiles and help each other when presented with a J, K and X.

The train dawdles out of Brisbane. Dawdles up to Gimpey. Dawdles to Bowen. Would I have been so keen to take the train if I'd read my *Lonely Planet* more thoroughly and known that this is a narrow-gauge railway, and carriages fall off the track if they try to hurtle round the bends? It is no use; I cannot pretend I organised this snail-train deliberately. But if Cath begins to realise the extent of my travelling ignorance, she keeps it to herself. I am quietly grateful for that.

Besides, it doesn't matter, we tell ourselves. We have plenty of time. We perch in our cramped pod and gaze out at the thirsty fields of Queensland: a brown, dusty landscape that seems to extend forever. There is no point in looking at our watches; hours become marinated; morning flows into afternoon which flows into evening without any attention to time. We drift into the restaurant car, to sit alongside a couple of bearded old soaks who are sharing one can of beer. A mother is playing with her children. Even here the conversation is muted, hushed as a doctor's waiting room.

The train slows at a station. There is sudden excitement, a buzz of policemen; guns are waving. For a second I wonder if I should throw myself to the floor, then realise that everyone else is pressed to the windows. Two minutes later an Aboriginal couple are pushed onto the platform: he is frantic, shouting, stabbing his fingers at nothing; a tall officer pushes him firmly into a seat. His partner, in a saggy rose-pink dress, weeps, flops heavily on a bench, agitated only when it becomes clear that they cannot continue their journey. She is accompanied back onto the train, emerging with a battered green suitcase and a couple of pillows. As the train pulls away the mother in the restaurant car pauses her colouring to explain that those people have broken the rules and so are not allowed to stay on the train.

If only it were as simple as broken rules. Their journey was important to them. Maybe someone is waiting for them. Or they are leaving something painful, unsafe, exploitative? Their journey must have meaning. I fill pages in my diary speculating on where they might be now, how they will manage being abandoned on that dusty platform, before I realise that I am beginning to ask questions about my own journey. I think I'll go back to the restaurant car and have a coke. I'm not ready for those questions yet. Okay, so I'm wallowing in ignorance. But my tinsel still glitters.

The relief of arriving in Cairns. My ears rumble with the rhythm of left-over train for several hours. I don't care. We've come here to swim in the Great Barrier Reef. Ever since I sat in the back of the geography lesson at school, picking chewing-gum from the underside of a wooden desk in a draughty classroom smelling of socks, and Miss Bloss pointing her nicotine-stained fingers at pictures of coral, I have wanted to come here.

'It's not as colourful/rich/vibrant as it used to be,' we have been told. I don't care. I just want to sink into tropical waters and be close to those miraculous corals, those magical fish.

I should, I know, care. The Barrier Reef is the largest coral reef in the world, the only living thing visible from space. In its nooks and crannies live the tiniest, rarest and most spectacular creatures. The Intergovernmental Panel on Climate Change has warned that the Reef could die. It is normal for variations in sea temperature to affect the lives of coral, but changes are continuing at such a rate that there is the risk of the sea becoming acidic, in which case the coral cannot survive. If the coral dies, the fish and molluscs that hide in its tentacles will disappear.

I know all this – and honestly, I care. (I can feel David Attenborough, breathless, on my shoulder. 'Think of the dolphins,' he whispers, 'the great sharks.') But on The Day, our Swimming Day, I swallow only excitement with my coffee as we sit by the wharf in the blue early morning light.

What would Miss Bloss say if she could see me now? She had a bullying approach to teaching; we learned unwillingly. Too many days spent cowering while she thumped her books on the desk in rhythm, 'Look at this work. You must be seriously lacking in grey matter.' Sounds ridiculous now; but it didn't make me laugh when I was thirteen. She's probably dead by now, which is a good thing, as I feel no need to thank her for introducing me to this.

We are surrounded by groups of beautiful young people, clutching diving gear (and each other). Cath has a sudden rush of nerves at the prospect of learning to snorkel among so many hormones. She need not have worried. We have selected a small boat for our trip, with a crew of three: Mark (sturdy, from Harpenden), Mark (tall and mousy-haired but far from mousy-natured, also from Harpenden), and Iris (from Germany).

We spend the morning chugging gently out onto the reef. The sea is magically blue, slapping against the side of the boat and filling the air with the scent of salt spray. Before long we are out of sight of land, the water clear and inviting beneath us and the azure sky above. Mark, Mark and Iris offer snorkelling lessons but I cannot think for excitement.

Sturdy Mark lures us into the water, with noodles (long foam sausages) and a floating ring to cling to if we need it. Flippers on, masks on, and we slip into the tropical waters. I have never snorkelled before, but the magic of the moment drowns nerves and within a minute or two I can drift away.

Warm water laps against my arms. All I can hear is the sigh of my breathing. All I can smell is the whiff of rubber in my mask. The snorkel rubs against my gums; I don't care.

How to describe the Barrier Reef? Great heaps of coral, a paintbox of blues and greens and yellows and purples and reds, dappled in midday sunlight, are home to creatures with great clam-like shells with disturbing mouth-parts. Lettuce-like tentacles waft in the current. Vibrant-blue starfish nestle in unlikely corners. Feelers from unseen bodies lurk in holes and crevices. I swim among fish, an ocean of fish, from bulky, motionless wrasse to iridescent green and blue parrotfish; shoals of tiny blue fish; large stripy fish with rude faces; transparent fish trying to hide against the sand; fish as curious about me as I am about them. I am a guest in this precious world.

I am the last to climb back in the boat for lunch. Mark, Mark and Iris open plastic boxes of salads, but I have forgotten my appetite. I can barely wait for our second swim, back in the comfort of the water and the magic of the reef.

Euphoria takes over. I cannot speak as we sail back towards Cairns.

Dreams are strange; some are best unattended as fulfilment brings only disappointment. Sod Miss Bloss. The rigidity of school was no preparation for this. The Barrier Reef overflows my expectations.

I fumble for words, then decide that some experiences are just too astonishing to be shaped into the confines of mere sentences.

Back in our cabin we unpack our towels. I have mislaid a pair of black knickers – left in the toilet when I changed, presumably. We speculate over the reaction of Mark, Mark and Iris.

7.

Next stop: New Zealand. The mechanics of packing and unpacking are beginning to feel familiar. Everything has its right place in my rucksack. The process is comforting, in a strange way. I can keep my rucksack tidy, even when there is no coherence in the rest of the world.

We take straightforward, if tedious, flights from Cairns to Brisbane to Auckland. My tinsel survives, and for a second I stroke it, touching my daughters. Stop it; this is no place for nostalgia.

We have to catch an early bus from Auckland to Rotorua, through rolling hillsides reminiscent of the calmer corners of Devon, arriving just before lunchtime to a stink of sulphur drowning our timely hunger. There is a stampede of young people grabbing rucksacks and making for the queue in the Tourist Information Centre. Like us, they have nowhere to stay.

Cath sits in a grey chair; for the first time she looks tired. Her hands, slightly swollen with the heat and effort of the journey, rest on her blue rucksack. She is, I remind myself, somebody's mother. I must look out for her. I seize a pile of leaflets as if I know what I'm doing and ring the first with a freephone number: Tresco.

'Good morning, sorry, afternoon. Do you have a twin room for four days, please?'

'Seems like you don't even know what day it is.' There is a jovial timbre in his reply; I try to place his accent: almost orthodox BBC but with a hint of Midland city in his vowels. 'I'm full today, but do have room from tomorrow. Tell you what, I've got a caravan you could have tonight and then come into the house tomorrow. I'm just driving back from the bus station now; why don't I come and pick you up – just a minute ...' The phone is muffled and there is a woolly conversation before he returns: 'I'll come and pick you up. You have a look, just to see if you like it; no problems if you don't.'

I explain the position to Cath. She stares at the accommodation queue.

'Good to know,' she says.

And so we meet Victor, a lanky, gangly man in his fifties with sparse hair and skin as grey as the rocks around the geysers. The drive to his guesthouse is delayed by a tour around the town with running commentary (here is the town hall and here are the hot springs and here is the spa, and what smell? You get used to the smell, you might like to go to the museum, most people seem impressed with that, and if you want we can arrange for you to go to a Maori evening – we can talk about that later, and there is a village on the edge of town, you might like that, too) before he telephones his wife to tell her there are two extra guests, two ladies, 'well I couldn't leave them standing in the bus station, could I?' He agrees that the caravan may need a bit of sorting out.

He lives in a bungalow, just ten minutes' walk from the town centre. We are led into a sitting room, with comfortable chairs around the edge and on the walls a collection of women's hats, a Harry Potter t-shirt and a pink basket. Cath has recovered from her weariness; she struggles with giggles when Victor invites us to admire an origami toadstool on the sideboard. I slurp my tea, which doesn't help. We have no time to think before Trinka, his wife, slides in and smiles through her dismay at finding so many people in her sitting room; she declares she will sort out the caravan and turns away.

We can wait in their spa; it is warmed by thermal water and is, initially, inviting. But the sides are stone, and slippery – we cannot work out if they are coated with paint or algae. And the water is almost too hot; within minutes we are uncomfortable. We resort to padding around the bungalow clutching towels, with Victor nattering after us, and Trinka busy.

At last – our room is ready. It is, we discover, the tiniest caravan we have ever seen; we have to change in relays. Cath mutters something about Wendy houses. I pretend to have a sense of humour. But we manage for one night before moving to a room in the bungalow.

Our stay in Rotorua is framed by Victor. I don't think I ever see him sit down, even when urging us into seats. He strides along his corridor, reminding me of a character created by Mervyn Peake with his clicking knees and elongated fingers. He minces between the chairs in his sitting room, props up walls. He has canny hearing, knows each time we come and go, offers chocolates and pours tea at every opportunity and entices us into conversation.

'You are lucky we are here,' he tells us, 'we had planned to return to Korea tomorrow, but the friends who had agreed to come and run this place have let us down; they won't be here until May, and so we must stay.' Yet there is no sign of packing.

'Good to know,' Cath says.

'Korea?' I ask.

'Trinka is from Korea. She would like to go home. We lived there before, but there was much sadness. Her family did not like her marrying a European ...'

'That must have been ... ' I am trying to make this sound like a discussion.

'They would not speak to us. It was hard for Trinka; all her family; no one would speak to her.' My subsequent experience suggests that marrying a European is a delight for most South-East Asian families as it promises affluence for them all.'We had a son there; he died; he had leukaemia and died. We had to leave; it was too sad to stay.'

'I'm sorry; it must have been ...' So why are they going back? And why now?

'Yes; so many memories; he was seventeen. I have other grandchildren, of course, but I never see them.' So were there earlier marriages? There are no photographs of children in the rooms we share; maybe they are clustered in their private spaces.

'But I cannot carry on much longer. I am ill, I have cancer and will not live much longer.' This might explain the pallid, clammy skin. 'And I have multiple sclerosis; that is why I stumble occasionally.' He seems no clumsier than the rest of us, but I have no medical skill to assess his dexterity. 'My brother, he had multiple sclerosis and he died. We were in real estate together but I gave that up when he died; that's when we came here.' I thought he said they were in Korea when their son died?

'You write?' He has noticed my diary, but makes no attempt to read it. 'I have written three books, but they cannot be published until their subjects have died.' (More dying?) 'I cannot print the truth yet. It would be too difficult for too many people.'

'You have the manuscripts?' I ask. This is the first writer I have met who did not seize on my diary and want to talk about writing.

'Oh yes, they are tucked away safely. One day everyone will know the truth. I did research for the British Government, but it cannot be told.' I try to find a question that might give more clues, but his mind has moved on.

'And I have seen a psychiatrist.' At last, something I might believe.

Yet, in spite of his strangeness, we do not feel threatened by him. There is none of the stomach-lurching I have felt with other older Europeans with young Asian brides. I would trust him with my daughters. He is a generous man, with his time and his tea and chocolates. He witters – we listen; it is a game we play and seems to keep him happy.

And Trinka is far from the timid Eastern woman we first thought her to be. She nurtures Victor with her hint-of-a-smile, nudging him from the room when he seems tired without paying attention to his possible frailty. There is profound affection behind her almond eyes. But even she cannot challenge him as he stops us one morning as we are about to head into town.

'Wait here,' he commands, disappearing briefly, returning at the far end of the corridor.

'No, stand there, and I'll walk towards you. Cath, you will know where this is.' We are staring at an unremarkable picture of a fishing village which Cath eventually recognises as the Scottish village of Pittenweem. It seems she has passed some sort of test, and she preens obligingly.

'Good to know,' she says.

Then Victor brings the picture nearer, urging us to look

closer; we realise it is a collage, a hotchpotch of fabric. Victor puffs with pride. This picture, he explains, is a collage of lingerie; the floral pattern of petticoat to represent the sea is, he insists, particularly fetching.

It is November 7th; I have been away for one month, and am staying with a man who delights in a picture made from women's underwear.

8.

We escape into the town. To the museum, where western, scientific, explanations of a major volcanic eruption are given equal weight to a Maori legend of an ogre, named Tama-o-hoi, who lived in the mountain and acted out his rage when visitors ate his sacred honey. Miss Bloss taught us about volcanoes; I am on the side of the ogre.

Curiosity stirred, we decide to visit Whakarewarewa, a Maori settlement on the outskirts of Rotorua. They make money from tourists, of course, but this is also a living village; its occupants work in the town and sustain a Maori way of life at home. (Ah, home. I cannot begin to think what I mean by home at the moment. Surely not Victor's? That other home – that Wiltshire home – is half a world away. It is buried in November, the air thick with bonfire smoke. It is Polly's graduation day. Her sisters will cheer for me.)

Here Maoris bathe together in the warm spring waters, steam food together in the hottest, sulphurous pools. They live in small wooden huts with no hint of hierarchy or rivalry. We wander around bubbling, glugging pools of mud, fizzy steams of eggy sulphur, geysers spouting boiling water several feet into the air. We admire the majestic meeting hall, with its intricate carvings. For lunch we eat corn which has spent the last couple of hours wallowing in boiling sulphuric pools; it is dripping in butter, sweet, delicious, with no hints of its pongy cooking.

All very educational. We even try to persuade ourselves that the reason we attend the display twice is to listen to their stories. They are, Cath agrees, good to know. We sit, dutifully, absorbing Maori legends, watching the dances. They are polished, practised, professional. And they finish with a *Haka* – which is meant to be terrifying, with all its smacking and stamping and sweaty male bodies. Maybe its true purpose is to excite the juices of rival women and entice them into changing sides.

I am converted.

My camera tells a more complicated story. Although there is a group of eight on stage, I have twenty pictures of one Maori; a striking young man with inviting eyes and fresh skin and muscles and a tattoo on his shoulder. His chest ripples; he slaps his knees as he performs the *Haka* is if they have offended him.

I want to walk my fingers down his back and pretend I am nineteen again. ('Mum, you can't say that!' I'm not sure if Anna is shocked or relieved that age doesn't bring a loss of interest. 'What if you were a bloke, looking at a young woman like that?' She is too persistent; too logical. I accept the rebuke, then return to my photographs. Maybe I should delete some of them, but not that one, nor that one ...)

It is not only me who is entranced by him (why am I still justifying myself?). During the first show some western men are invited on stage to learn how to perform a *Haka*. They are comically pathetic – but they know it, find themselves funny, and so no feelings are hurt. In the afternoon women can learn to swing a poi. Cath needs no second invitation, scurrying to the stage to make sure she has a place. She arranges herself on the stage next to that Maori, allowing him to brush against her as her poi swings wildly in the opposite direction from everyone else's.

She asks for copies of my pictures.

9.

It is time to head south. An agent meets us at the airport in Christchurch, taking us to meet our campervan. Already Cath is goggle-eyed. She has never driven anything bigger than her Nissan Micra, and her insurance company laughed at her suggestion she might be allowed to drive a campervan. It is a cruel reminder of the difference in our ages. We are led to the biggest vehicle we have ever seen: a des res of a campervan, with two bedrooms, kitchen, living/dining room, bathroom, with a cab attached at the front. A mobile bungalow of a campervan. Why so huge? When we met to organise this part of the trip, and were shown campervan plans, the two-berth options were illustrated with a double bed. One night at Victor's we could manage, but more than three weeks was asking too much of us both; I had insisted on separate beds without realising the enormity of the vehicle we would end up with.

Cath stands beside me, clammy, appalled. We ignore the slight smell of damp, noticing only that it is impossibly clean. I stiffen my shoulders; one of us must appear to know what we are doing. I listen to instructions as if two weeks away from my 'A' levels in campervan management. Water here; electricity there; this is how you empty the toilet; don't forget to turn the gas off before you drive anywhere. Remember to steer a wide sweep around the bends: you have seven metres of van behind you.

'Good to know,' Cath says. Somehow it comforts her.

This is no time to remind myself I have never driven anything bigger than an Audi. Before that – old Renaults, a Ford of some kind (I'm not a car person), back to my rusting Morris Minor, with its hole on the passenger side floor and rattle from the gearbox I elected not to explore. I bought my Morris Minor on the day I passed my driving test. And drove straight from the garage into Stroud High Street and off into the Cotswolds. I don't remember being alarmed then. I don't even remember worrying about insurance or traffic or the challenge of hills. If I could do that when I was twenty-four, surely I could manage this in my sensible years.

Besides, Cath is frightened enough for both of us.

Within an hour of reaching the campsite I can recall only the slightest details of that short journey. I negotiated the car park at the supermarket where we stocked up with tea, coffee and wine. I turned into a cul-de-sac (another mistake) and reversed into a driveway. I manoeuvred into the furthest corner of the campsite. Cath spent most of the journey in silence.

She cooks jacket potato; we spit anxiety at each other. We must make friends with the van somehow; I decide we must give it a name. Cath is unconvinced, but we agree on Bertha. Conversation drifts between attention to poor Bertha and equally obsessive avoidance of the subject. Night closes in. I climb into the space above the cab and make a nest. Rain hammers on the roof; my nose is cold; I can hear Cath shuffling in her narrow bed next to the cooker while the campervan grows to the size of a semi-detached house in my imagination.

The next morning it takes fifteen minutes to extricate ourselves from our berth in the campsite. Fortunately we are the last to leave and no one is watching.

But, within half an hour, I begin to relish the prospect of travelling with our home behind us. The engine growls and surges beneath my feet; I feel an unexpected sense of power staring down at the road from such an unfamiliar height. The world, it seems, is literally beneath us. I am so smug I want to sing. Cath shuts me up with poetry.

We – Bertha, Cath and I – will have three weeks together. Traffic in New Zealand is thankfully orderly, predictable, and sparse. The road system is efficient. Large notices on bends indicate their maximum speed and I slow down obediently. Only twice do I take them a little fast, and Cath is polite enough to say nothing although the whites of her knuckles tell

39

me all I need to know. I never quite master the art of long slow descents without over-reliance on the brakes. When we stop to admire the tumbling river on the Haast Pass Bertha responds with the sharp smell of hot metal; we wait for the brakes to cool and no harm is done. We take one unnecessary short cut, through the highest pass in the Southern Alps; I negotiate bend after bend, not daring to look up nor down, nor at Cath's repetitive finger-tapping on the door-frame. Invitations to pull over to put on snow chains (as if we know how) are not encouraging. But when we stop at the top, we drink in a view down to the bluest of lakes and across the valley to the snow-tipped Crown Range. The air is thin, but there is warmth in the sun and the sky is almost cloudless. Is it worth the driving alarms? Of course it is.

Just once, two days before Bertha is due back in Christchurch, does she let us down. It has rained, persistently, for days. Water drips, first through a small cupboard, and then through the hood above the cooker. The electricity fails. I am not sure how we can keep warm. We spend one chilly night wearing everything we own and snuggled in all the blankets we can find. But the next day our clothes are damp and even our bones are cold.

Protracted sogginess might be manageable for the young but is foolish for the ripe and wrinkled. Although I cannot tell her, I feel an uncomfortable responsibility for Cath; I need to send her home to her daughter unscathed. If Bertha can't be coaxed into action in the morning we must admit defeat, ring the agents and find somewhere dry for tonight. We wrap ourselves in as many layers as we can muster, climb into the cab and I turn the key to the engine. It growls, hopefully, beneath us and Bertha springs into life, smacking my pessimism in the face. Thelma and Louise – pah! We sing all the way towards Christchurch. In the next campsite we manage to reconnect electricity, turn the heating up high and fan our faces in the relief of hot air.

In three weeks we will take Bertha home, and I will be

absurdly proud to return her in the same pristine condition in which she was given to us. In spite of her size, which Cath never quite forgives her for, I grow quite attached. I admit to surges of unladylike feelings of power as I urge her up the steepest hills or round the tightest corners. When I left home I wondered if I could travel alone. I'm no further forward with that conundrum, but at least I know I can drive a truck now.

Nevertheless, I relish the prospect of a real bed.

10.

They prove to be an eventful three weeks.

Postcards from South Island, New Zealand do not lie. It is painfully beautiful. The Southern Alps are the spine of the island. They tower above the ocean to the west, spilling glaciers like icing towards the sea. The terrain is fierce beyond the tree line, with harsh outcrops and rocky corners. Snow towers on mountain tops, thick and icy in some places, smattered like sugar in others.

Rivers tumble into glorious lakes. Geologists (and Miss Bloss) tell us that their extraordinary colour is the result of mica and other minerals washed down by glaciers. In the early morning they are a pale, milky-blue; as the sun rises they become a sea of cornflower; if clouds threaten they wear an elegant blue-grey. Water shushes over gravel; birds twitter unseen. Crowds of yellow lupins play along the water's edge. We breathe the cleanest, sweetest air.

My camera steams from over-use. I am tempted, each time we turn a corner, to pull into the side of the road to take pictures. But photographs cannot encompass this astonishing scenery. Written descriptions cannot do it justice – my diary overflows with the word 'beautiful'. Cath searches for poetry, but even lyricists struggle to describe the feelings that sweep through us as, over the brow of every hill and around every bend, we are greeted with another view to make us gasp.

They make me want to sing, and shout, and sting me into silence – all at the same time.

Wiltshire is beautiful, too, in its quiet way. It feels to me like a forgotten county, to be raced through on the way to Devon and Cornwall, leaving the rolling Downs and mysteries of Savernake Forest for those of us who live here. There is a tree in the forest that is over one thousand years old; it sprouted its first tender leaves before William the Conqueror landed in Hastings. Pollarding has left it gnarled, distorted, with ancient branches needing the same support my old aunt gets from her walking frame. Before embarking on this trip I would walk there sometimes, find comfort from its longevity. My stomach-churning worries seemed insignificant beside something that had survived for so long. But too often it rained, and I scuttled back through soggy leaves to face the reality of packing.

New Zealand is even beautiful in the rain. And the snow. And the wind. And the hail. Which is a good thing, because we experience them all. Rarely at the same time, and only – towards the end of the trip – for days at a time. But, mostly, we refuse to become obsessively British about it. We don waterproofs and plod on regardless. We spend just one morning under duvets reading books while thunder rages around us and Bertha rocks in the gale.

We time our walks carefully. We grab a break in the clouds to head into the mountains; Cath wanders around the shores of Diamond Lake, while I stroll up the Rob Roy Track to the glaciers. I have been assured that this is a gentle walk, with views of the glacier to aim for. I leave the wide green waters of the Matukituki River. The Rob Roy stream thunders along beside me, stumbling over stones and boulders and fallen trees; its roar, in places, even defeating the birds. When the path edges away a little I can hear the little hoot of the bell bird, the teet-teet of the tiny rifleman, but soon I am back to the tumble of water. In spite of whiffs of mud and moss and bog the air feels sweetly clean; I want to drink it.

But it is definitely not a gentle walk. I look again at the map, looking for contours that might have warned me that this is steep. No contours, only dots marking heights above sea-level that I have ignored.

I climb over one thousand feet, not a steady plod that my puffing lungs can get used to, but a scramble over rocks and muddy tree-roots, a clinging to branches to steady myself on narrow ledges where the path considers whether to sink into the river below, a paddle through streams swollen by recent rains. I try muttering some of Cath's poetry (Does the road wind uphill all the way?/Yes, to the very end ...), but it only makes me puff even harder. I refuse to remind myself that I am on my own, perched half way up a mountain; only Cath has any idea where I am and if a rescue team were reliant on her map-reading it would be next year before anyone found me. Instead I obsess about the challenge of climbing back down this path. Clambering up is one thing; I shall have to come down on my bottom.

My reward is worth every puff and scramble: the mucky mouth of the glacier, and a close encounter with a kea. Keas are parrot-like birds that have learned to exploit tourists with all the expertise of an entrepreneur. This one fancies my sandwich; his friend, puffing his feathers and pretending to be a chick, is his accomplice. The plot: the 'youngster' appeals to my camera, distracting me while the second steals my food. He has already negotiated the zip on my backpack and is clearly accomplished with plastic bags.

Do I sacrifice my lunch and take a photograph? There is, I confess, some undignified scrambling while I manage both (my stomach and I are looking forward to this sandwich). Only when it is clear they will get little more than crumbs does the chick-actor shake himself into clearly adult plumage, screeches 'kee-a' and soars into the sky. Within minutes they are back; a second group of hikers have arrived and are rustling wrappers. Should I warn them? Or enjoy the entertainment as they, too, scuttle between sandwiches and cameras?

My second walk takes me into the hills above Hanmer Springs in search of a waterfall. I stride through dappled forest tracks, dripping from yesterday's water and smelling of wet leaves. There is storm-debris everywhere – fallen trees, paths littered with pungent wood-shavings and scattered where logs have already been crudely cleared.

From time to time I sniff hints of soggy cinders. I wade across a shallow river crossing, glacial water chilly on my bare feet, then scramble along a muddy track to the clamour of the waterfall: a single stream falling over a hundred feet through the forest. The rain has crept in, but feels irrelevant. I can drive a campervan, negotiate keas, wade through rivers; for an hour I revel in an invincibility that discounts my age.

I need a passing Australian couple to bring me down to earth. I am about to set off back to the town along the high track when the man tugs my sleeve, points to the cloud and urges me to return through the forest.

'Don't take chances, not in this weather. Besides you won't see anything, not in this cloud.'

Did I learn nothing in Manly? He is right; rain hammers on the rock face and only a fool would contemplate the high path.

They call after me, 'You're from the campsite? With your mother?' I nod; I can't see the point of friend's mother explanations. 'You can't walk all the way back in this. We've got a car – wait for us at the bottom of the path. We'll take a few photos and be right behind you.'

I peer through the curtain of rain and accept.

I splash, slither, stride, splodge through rising mud back to the car park to wait beneath a sharp-smelling pine tree. Water drips down my neck. I resort to stamping my feet in a futile effort to keep warm, reminding myself that, only an hour ago, I was enjoying this. If I'd wanted to get cold and wet I could have stayed at home, trekked through Savernake Forest in December. I try not to shiver when they arrive, and we all flop gratefully into the dry of the car.

He flicks the ignition; and is met with a worthless click. They exchange a glance; I dare not speak. There is more flicking, more clicking. He groans, sinks his head onto the steering wheel.

'The light,' he says, 'we left the lights on. We've no battery. There's a notice at the bottom of the track, telling people to put their lights on; it's crazy, you don't need lights here; everyone must do this.'

It seems to be the fault of the notice.

We try to jump-start by rolling backwards down the hill. I duck my head down and can see nothing but trees rushing by, hear nothing but swishing wheels and the coughing engine. I have a sudden image of myself, with my sore knees and rats-tail-hair, curled on the back seat of a car owned by total strangers, in the middle of who knows where. A passer-by might have wondered if I was being kidnapped.

The car judders, coughs, and refuses to start. Too soon they see another car coming towards us (from my cocoon on the back seat I can see nothing); we are in the middle of the track, facing uphill. Time to unfurl, climb out of the car, and help push, pull and otherwise manipulate the car until it is facing downhill. I am given the pushing-place behind the back wheel, in the firing line for mud flying from beneath the impotent tyres.

The man, whose tight lips confirm he has no inkling that there might be a funny side to all this, resumes the driving; we slither on for another twenty yards or so, but the engine still refuses to fire, and we reach a dip in the road. Our combined strength is not enough to push this heavy car up a slope.

The rain is persistent, penetrative. My waterproof lives up to its name but my trousers are soaked through; mud is spattered on every item of clothing as well as my face and hands. I remind myself, grimly, that I gave myself permission to take risks.

'Bloody hire cars,' the man announces, 'they never have jumper leads. At home we always have jumper leads, never go out without them.' (Jumper, I realise, is Australia-speak for jump.)

Now it is the car hire company who is to blame. There is little discussion; his partner is deposited in the driving seat while we walk down the hillside, aiming for the village. There is no question: I must go with him; I have a map and can read it. He is far too grumpy for me to feel comfortable asking his name now.

Maps in New Zealand are generally accurate – but not drawn to scale. My directions would suggest that it is not far. We reach the gravel track, where the limited shelter offered by the trees cannot reach us. The stream, so delightful earlier, is now rushing, noisy, knee-deep; my fingers are too numb to untie my laces and I can feel him stamping his feet with impatience at my clumsiness. My knees take another opportunity to remind me of my age and twinge with every step. I tell myself firmly not to hobble.

There is no desultory conversation to fill the wet space between us. It is three miles to the road, and the nearest campsite, where an angular woman greets us as if soggy people arrive at her door every day. I want to hug her for the generosity of her welcome, but my colleague is too busy pressing her to search for jumper leads. She cannot find them, but she phones a garage and rescue is on its way.

I make it back to Bertha eventually and Cath behaves like a mother. I am cold and wet and let her. She makes steaming hot chocolate, dispatches me for a shower while it cools, provides ibuprofen for my aching knees, and sorts my sodden clothes. The radio in the shower block plays 'I'm Dreaming of a White Christmas'. I sing along. I have been cold, wet, and lost, even (I will admit it now) a little alarmed; but suddenly I am exhilarated. I have come a long way since Manly.

11.

It is difficult to imagine this wild landscape when it was alive with gold prospectors. We feel heroic, yet we have a campervan the size of a house and money to buy food. After hearing horror stories of vans with their brakes burning on the drive down the mountainside towards the sea, we even join a tour group to savour the rigours of Milford Sound. I am happy to have a few days that are less intrepid. I have made it to the other side of the world. I don't need to frighten myself on a regular basis, just to make the point that I'm actually travelling.

We both read Rose Tremain's *The Colour* before this trip. Set in the days of early exploration for New Zealand's gold, it is a tale of young people lured by the whiff of treasure; they struggled across mountains in freezing cold, set up in camps beside unkind rivers. It is not a journey many young people attempt today – though my brother's stories of crossing the Khyber Pass come close.

Literary curiosity sends us across a rickety bridge and into an old mining centre clinging to the rocky hillside outside Queenstown. It is a mine-museum now, and we stroll along the guided walks and sanitised pathways. But the cruel lives of prospectors, and their fantasies of fortunes buried in these rocks, linger in the huts and crannies. Rose Tremain did not exaggerate the harshness of life in the mines. Bertha feels positively luxurious.

But there were fortunes to be made – and spent. We pause on the west coast to explore Hokitika. The town was portal to the western gold rush. Eighty hotels were built here in two years. Boats jostled for space in the port; the town exploded with bawdy exploitation. It was the gateway for prospectors seeking fortunes, and the town to which they returned with bulging pockets.

Now we are the only van on the campsite.

'No orgies tonight then,' Cath says.

'Good to know,' I reply.

It is a bleak, lonely town. The streets are almost empty. Even the jewellers look lost without customers. There is a rancid smell of running sea. Dust flies across street corners. We need shelter and head for the museum. Among the paraphernalia that has survived from the mining days we find the story of Barbara Weldon.

Barbara Weldon was born in Ireland, but the date is unknown. She must, at some stage, have made it to England as she is next recorded as travelling from Liverpool to Melbourne – no explanation is given for this trip but Australia was, at that time, used as a dumping ground for Britain's unwanted. From Melbourne she was sent to Hokitika on a one-way ticket for 'using obscene language in a public place' – the details far to delicate to be recorded in a public museum. There are descriptions of her as 'sickly-looking'. Her occupation is 'unclassified', presumably a euphemism for prostitution.

This narrative does not record the number of times she was back in court, with convictions for drunkenness, disorderly behaviour, vagrancy, soliciting and attempted suicide. In 1870 she tried to drown herself in the river; in 1882 her body was found in a burnt-out house.

I'm not sure why this story upsets me. Neither *Google* nor *Wikipedia* can give me any more details that the few sentences I scribble in my notebook. I want to make some sort of memorial to her; to embellish her story and make her breathe. I want her to have lovers, to have the best possible reason to 'use obscene language in a public place'. When John, my husband, died I used after-the-watershed language, often, and in very public places; I overdid the wine; fantasised about driving my car into pillars on the motorway. Anna, Tessa, Annie, Polly – all put their arms around me.

My life reshaped, as lives do. Nobody sent me to New Zealand. I came because I wanted to.

12.

Cath and I have said tearful farewells. I am on my own again. I understand alone. I've lived alone for eleven years, and grown to relish solitude. There were rearrangements, of course, when John died. He used to bring me a cup of tea in bed every morning; waking in cold sheets with no tea was such a brutal introduction to each day I invested in a small kettle for the bedroom. Such temporal adjustments gave my disordered feelings space to settle into new places.

In time I grew to enjoy the slight shove needed to close my front door; a shutting out of the world; the cocoon of my own home. Friends and daughters were never far away; if I simply needed company I could drift to a nearby café.

But I begin to realise that the aloneness of travelling is different. There is no front door to close, no place to retreat other than a faceless room in a hotel or hostel. I have been away so long that these hostels begin to merge. There is no spreading of belongings around the room in an attempt to make it look as if I live in it. I have nothing but myself – and my precious notebook – to fall back on.

I spend hours scribbling, trying to work out how I feel about being alone like this. Not that the scribbling gets me anywhere. I am, very slightly, out of control. I can carry my body around more or less successfully; but my mind, I realise, still doesn't have the faintest idea what I'm doing.

I am in public spaces almost all the time. But I am not a public person – not only because I know nobody and so most conversations are largely trivial, but also, as a middle-aged woman, I am invisible. No one is curious about me. There are few conversations in Christchurch.

I organise my day (I shall go to the gardens, pause in the perfumed rose garden and try not to think of the blowsy roses that drop their petals in my own little garden at home. Then I will stop for lunch in a little café, maybe a museum in the afternoon, by which time ...). It is not difficult to fill time;

Christchurch provides plenty of opportunities. Doing challenges the creep of loneliness.

Nevertheless, the contradictions of invisibility weigh heavily here. I relish the new; but miss having someone to answer me back. Especially, Cath.

Which is probably why I float into conversation with two women on the Trans-Coastal Scenic train. We are all heading for the North Island.

'I'm glad we're sitting with someone we can talk to, not someone stuffy, aren't you Meg?' Meg, a blowsy, full-bosomed woman, around my age and with competent make-up, perfect nails and a hint of expensive perfume, nods in reply.

'I'm Elizabeth,' her friend persists. She is a thin, beige woman, clean-skinned and with her hair dyed an unconvincing copper. I offer my name and wait. Their story emerges in pieces. They are Australian, sisters-in-law having married two brothers; both marriages failed and each married again and were subsequently widowed. At first I think we are connected by parallel stories, but have no wish to get into a grieving discussion.

'Where exactly are you from?' I ask, ready to contribute anecdotes from my brief experience of Australia.

'Now, my second husband, he was dying when I married him.' Elizabeth chooses to ignore me. 'Only six months we had but it was the best thing I done. Now my grandchildren, see,' – Elizabeth puffs her ineffectual chest briefly – 'well I've got five children, and eighteen grandchildren, and, well we see a lot of them, so it's nice for them. And I've always been around kiddies, I was a dinner lady, and I drove one of them buses, but not now. I get out of course, I mean I'm seventy now, and I've got the animals.'

I stare out of the window while she counts her dogs and ducks and chooks; she sells eggs she tells me, and vegetables – they've helped pay for this trip.

There is a sudden change of subject. 'I don't know if you'd noticed,' – Elizabeth irritates a spot on her upper lip – 'this is really sore. I think I might have a bit of grit in it, what do you think, Meg?'

Meg is dragged into the conversation. 'See how it goes. Don't think it's as bad as my foot.' She produces a bandaged foot and waits for me. With no injury of my own my contribution to the discussion is obviously limited.

'Fell, didn't I? Almost ripped my toenail off. Doctor charged NZ$60 dollars just to put a bandage on. Means I can't wear my proper shoes, and I'm stuck with these sandals.' The sandals look functional to me, but I can see that they are slightly out of place alongside the elegance of her dress and immaculate make-up.

'Me, I have to go to the doctor all the time.' Elizabeth must join in. 'I've got a heart valve and cholesterol; can't eat cheese or I'll have a stroke and that'll be bloody expensive over here.' I don't even have an interesting illness to talk about.

Meg flips open her phone, presses some buttons and purses her lips.

'Put that bloody thing away.' Elizabeth turns to me. 'She's got a fella, see, that's why we're here. But he's not, well, he's not free.' She stumbles over "free", leans her face in a sideways fashion as if trying, and failing, to wink.

'This is It,' Meg assures me, ignoring her friend's pursed lips. Her cheeks are pink and she cannot hold back the grin that transforms her face into embarrassed delight. 'I never thought it would happen, but this is It.' They met last year, she tells me, when he was working in Australia, and have been in touch ever since. I realise that she is checking her phone every twenty minutes. She rings him, leaves a message.

'That's why we're here, see.' Elizabeth gathers me into the conspiracy. 'He said come over, so she asked me to travel with her cos it wouldn't look right if she came on her own. I said "yes", though it was a bloody struggle finding the money. And I insisted we saw more than her hotel room while we're here – so we've been on a ten-day bus tour down South, and now we're heading back to Auckland, to see him.'

Meg is still flipping her phone.

'No point in sending a message; you know he's working. Besides,' – Elizabeth turns to me, her voice suddenly brittle – 'he's got a wife. So we have to sit and wait for him to call.'

'You don't get it,' Meg retorts. 'She's frail, he can't leave her, I understand that. They haven't had sex for seventeen years. This is the same for him as it is for me; there's never been anything quite like this, and when we are together it's just, well, just ...'

Elizabeth flicks her eyes towards the ceiling and sighs. Meg checks again, to find a message from *Vodaphone*: she has no more money on the phone.

'Good.' Elizabeth is triumphant. 'Maybe now you'll put the bloody thing away.'

Meg escapes to the toilet.

'Making a bloody fool of herself, I mean, look at her.' Elizabeth leans towards me. I cannot sink any further into my chair. 'It takes her half an hour to put all that slap on, and who does she think she's fooling. She's drooling over some bloke who's probably done this time and time again. I mean, he even asked me once if I'd like him to help me out, if you know what I mean! Didn't tell her, of course, but that's the type of man he is. She just don't see it.' I feel as if I am in a strange play and have forgotten my lines.

Meg returns, full of smiles. She can buy a top-up card in Picton, before we catch the ferry. But there is no message before we sail, and it is only minutes before we are beyond reach of a signal.

The wind in the Cook Strait is fierce – by British landlubber standards. I stand at the back of the ferry, hair imprisoned in a scarf, revelling in its uncomplicated energy. The two women stand beside me, faces in rigid grimace, before seeking shelter inside. I watch as the horizon slides from green to blue.

I wish I could stand there forever, clutching the icy railings, wind distorting my cheeks. I need the wind to blow away the taste of their mutual bitterness. But the cold, eventually, drives me inside. Meg and Elizabeth have saved a space for me; the conversation is in full spit.

'I wish you wouldn't read out those texts,' Elizabeth is saying. She turns to me as if I had been sitting there all the time. 'I never knew women could talk like that. And on the phone, she talks like I'm not there, well, like men in a bar.' She cannot stop. Meg makes a second visit to the toilet.

'It's all she does, Michael this, Michael that (the first time I've been offered a name). All this 'my poor wife' bit; she just laps it up. We flew to Auckland so she could see him, we waited in the hotel for him to phone, I went downstairs for a couple of hours when he turned up, then we waited for him to phone again. This is meant to be my holiday. I don't know why I came.'

Meg returns and it is Elizabeth's turn for the loo.

'She doesn't get it, does she?' Meg looks to me for an ally. 'Just bitter, I suppose. Old and bitter. Dried up. She doesn't see that this is the most wonderful thing that could happen to me – and to Michael – and one day we will be together, but it has to be like this for a while.'

I am exhausted from listening. I cannot decide if they are humorous or tragic; maybe both. I lose them, somehow, in the scramble for luggage in Wellington, and find relief in solitude.

PART THREE

TIKA TO THE RESCUE

13.

It is time to leave the safety of a common language and launch into less chartered waters. I spend my last night awake. My stomach knots with alarm; this is the step I had thought I was looking forward to, but now I am quivering with apprehension. Tomorrow I will fly from Auckland to Brisbane, from Brisbane to Bangkok, from Bangkok to Kathmandu. On my own.

Before I set off (it feels like months ago now, though it's less than two) I pondered, too briefly perhaps, on my capacity to travel alone. Now I have put myself in the position of having no choice. I risk dreaming of home; the Christmas lights will be twinkling in the High Street; I'd have my curtains closed against the fog. But it is a fog I know, and understand, can negotiate with predictable caution. I know the ways of Wiltshire. Am I really going to look back on this, when I'm eighty, and be pleased I did it?

Wiltshire is no preparation for the shock of Kathmandu. I drift into the red-brick arrivals hall, smelling of dust and travelling, and stand by the creaking carousel. My rucksack appears. It has lost only one strand of tinsel on its journey, and I am – too briefly – elated. But there is no air-conditioned hall to stroll into, no line of polite drivers clutching boards with names written on them. Instead I am spat out into stark midday sunshine: it is a shocking light, reflecting off every car window, every grain of dust. A sea of Nepali faces crashes over me; cries of 'taxi, taxi' and 'hotel, hotel.' Everything is discordant, loud, dazzling, like a piece of modern music with a tune hiding somewhere just out of reach. I cling to a railing and fight an urge to retreat. Even the bleak arrivals hall would be more comforting than this.

'Tika.' My voice is feeble. Tika is a guide from Pokhara, recommended by a friend of a friend; he has promised to be here, to soften the Asian landing just a little. I cough, try louder: 'Tika.'

'You want Tika?' I hear the voice but cannot connect it with one of the faces in front of me. I nod.

'Stand still – in this corner. He will find you.' I do as I'm told, and, as promised, Tika's beaming face emerges from the hordes. I resist a western urge to fling my arms round him, manage a discreet *namaste*, and he leads me to the taxi. It seems that the man who had told me to wait was our taxi driver; I was unaware of him quietly watching for my safety until Tika arrived.

Tika is a healthy man, slightly-built like many Nepali, and with eyes that seem to smile even when his wide mouth is solemn. I trust him instantly. But then I know I would disintegrate without him.

As we climb into the taxi he removes his plaid hat, and wipes his hands across the bristles on his head.

'My uncle,' he explains, 'he has died. So I must shave my head; it is what men do here when someone has died. I do not always have no hair, yes.'

I assure him his lack of hair is no problem.

'Once I had this haircut in England. When I visit Emma (the friend of the friend), I thought a number one cut meant it was the best. And I come out looking like this, yes.'

Suddenly he bursts into giggles. He is laughing for both of us, I think.

He takes me to a hotel.

'And you, where are you staying?' I ask.

'I have places to stay here friends, yes,' he explains.

'And you have places to eat – I need you to guide me, but you must eat good food, too, stay in reasonable places. I don't want you in some scruffy annex while I have a comfortable room.'

I have not, yet, learned the contours of his face, and cannot tell if this surprises him. Nor do I have any idea if such arrangements are the norm. But I had not realised how important this is to me until I met him. He is my guide, not a servant. He raises his eyebrows at me; he seems to be asking a question but I'm not sure what it is. I shrug some sort of reply.

We abandon my rucksack in the hotel and he leads me out into through a maze of tiny streets to Durbar Square. I follow, linked by an unseen umbilical; without it I would probably cry. There is bustling, shuffling, scurrying, a maelstrom of people and colours and buildings and dust. There are tiny shops and street stalls wherever I look: spices, vegetables, saris, rugs, hangings, incense. I reel from an olfactory bombardment: turmeric, paprika, the stink of incense, sweet popcorn. Nepali shops, spilling cooking pots and sacks of rice into the street, rub shoulders with trekking shops with their sleeping bags and backpacks. Hawkers press me to buy pots of tiger balm and wooden chess sets. We pass a market, where women are squatting beside mat-loads of vegetables, bowls of nutmeg, paneer; a small butcher's with a white slab, about waist-high, at the front with a heap of rancid chicken-bits and a pile of something red and bloody and buzzing with flies. Sari shops fly glorious fabric, like kites. There are cows, the occasional mangy dog, the euk of hawking and spitting, endless coughing. Taxis hoot; bike-bells ring. The taste of traffic creeps down my throat.

I am light-headed in my lack of understanding. Tika lures me into another market. I never tire of markets. The smell and the noise, the heart of them. The feeling that they are at the centre of everything living in a town or village. Well, maybe I should qualify that. My local market is polite, dignified even, when compared with the pandemonium of Kathmandu. At home I wouldn't dream of bartering over the price of apples or cheese. Here, I am seduced into thinking I might need a colourful this or pungent that, spices and vegetables I cannot recognise and have no way of cooking but tempt me anyway.

Tika grins at me, shakes his head. I am behaving like a tourist and of course it makes him laugh. There is something about Tika laughing that makes joining in compulsory.

14.

I'm tired, which makes me sound feeble but there it is. I have been on the move for weeks, and recognise a need for my feelings to catch up with my body. And my body, too, needs respite.

Young people seem able to race from place to place, with bottomless energy. Pokhara, almost two hundred kilometres west of Kathmandu, is a ten-day refuge from restlessness. Tika lives here; he sinks into his family and I wallow in the peace of Phewa Lake, taking time to gather my thinking, to revisit those questions that launched this voyage.

Only to find that they don't matter so much, now I'm here. I am learning to allow my feelings to fluctuate. Some days I bounce along the streets, willingly tempted into small shops to admire exotic paintings, glittery wall-hangings, flimsy clothes. 'Om mani padme hum', a traditional Buddhist chant, seeps from every doorway, and I find myself humming along with it.

I am an outsider, of course, but the Nepali are universally welcoming and overlook my social clumsiness. My diary overflows with question marks, but there feels less need to find solutions. Indeed, the questions are more muted now; I begin to turn my attention to where this journey might lead me. And today it leads me by the water as it sinks from blue to purple in the evening light, in air smelling of mountains and with the high snow dressed in evening pink.

There are, of course, other times when the sensory overload feels overwhelming and I have to resist an urge to creep back to my hotel room. Who is to notice if I stay in bed for a day? Read, write, doze.

But I don't. An old parental dictum resounds in my head: you didn't come all this way just to lie about. A dictum with a Reggie Perrin quality. Nevertheless, I don't lie about; I dress as if I mean it, and head for the lakeside. I'm not yet brave enough to try catching a bus on my own, but am happy to wander beside the water. There the gentle lapping, and the shadows of the mighty Annapurna, soothe me. It is, of course, worth getting up.

On occasional energetic days Tika takes me walking. I ask endless questions about Nepal, its culture, its people.

'We have a new constitution.' He says this with more pride than any western man with a new car. After years of civil unrest the king has finally stepped down. 'There will be elections, democracy.' His eyes are shining; he is passionate about politics.

'Education for everyone. Especially for our women. Many men are gone, to the cities, to Kathmandu, to India, to the Middle East. Women work on the farms. They must read, then teach their children.'

I had not expected a Nepali feminist. 'Nepali women, so strong. In the civil war the men, they run away to the cities, hide in the mountains, take to drinking. The women stay, grow the vegetables, look after the children.'

'I have one daughter,' he tells me. 'I can afford for her education, yes. I will not have two children till I can pay for education, yes.'

Later I will meet his daughter. She only has to grin at him and he collapses in paternal adoration. She is bright, and feisty, and naughty. His Amazon woman, aged seven.

*

Tika also uses our walks as an opportunity to visit relations scattered across these foothills of the Annapurna mountain range. On Christmas Day we head across a wobbly bridge and up a stony track to the village of Dopahare. We pass a group of women, gathered beneath a tree.

'They are co-operative, yes,' Tika explains. 'They borrow money together to buy seeds and sell vegetables.'

'Always the women?' I ask.

'Of course.' I have asked a stupid question.

We leave them to their deliberations. Further down the path I lean on my trekking pole to catch my breath, pretending it is simply a manoeuvre to make space for a woman in a ragged crimson sari tripping down the mountainside, bent beneath a basket of satsumas (known as oranges here). We buy two, then walk to a small temple to admire the mountains and eat them. Across the track is a shack, where an elderly couple lean against the doorway. They cannot take their eyes off me. Eventually the woman hobbles across the road; she gives us more oranges.

Tika translates their conversation. 'Why is she (meaning me) walking? Why does she not take the bus?'

'She likes to walk. In her country they walk for pleasure.' A look of sheer mystery crosses her face. Tika shrugs. He, like them, probably thinks I'm slightly mad.

On we plod, pausing by a school playground where children chatter and two women sit in a corner marking what seem to be exam papers. Again I am the object of inquiry; children gather to feel the skin of my arms and the silk of my hair. Too soon it is time for them to return to their lessons.

Tika is stern. 'Off you go – if you don't she'll take you away and you'll never come home again!'

They scatter to a distance of about ten feet, not quite sure if they should believe him. For a moment I want to protest; after all, I have an enhanced Criminal Records check. I spent my working life keeping children safe. Then pause, swallow my arrogance; such warnings used to be given to white children unfamiliar with black people. Maybe there is grim justice in such a turnaround.

It is a relief to reach Tika's aunt's tiny farm. I have spent too much of the morning pretending not to puff in the thin mountain air. Tika shows me sheds, the biogas tank. An animal I take to be a cow stirs in her byre, warning us away from her calf with a low moo.

'No, she is water buffalo, yes,' Tika says. With that he launches into mimicking the comparative moos of cow and water buffaloes. It is important I can tell the difference, he tells me, as water buffaloes do not like tourists. His moos echo across the valley, answered by an animal miles away. I must copy; my moos are feeble and there is no reply. Again and again I fail the test of distinguishing one moo for another, possibly because I am laughing too hard. I am a poor pupil. But he does not send me to the back of the class.

Meanwhile his aunt searches for stones in the rice, and then cooks us a Christmas dinner of spinach and dhal. With oranges to follow.

Eventually we slither on down the hillside, along a marble path that never sees the sun, still slippery from recent rain. As I cling to my trekking pole with one hand and Tika with the other – the only way I can stay upright – a group of women in pink and blue flip-flops stride the other way. Tika seems to know them all. He grins all the way to the valley floor and then cannot resist translating their conversation:

'They asked me how old you are. I told them you are seventy! They said you are doing really well for your age!' He chortles his delight. Before leaving home I wondered how local people would respond to me: today one thinks I'm bonkers for enjoying a walk, I've eaten five oranges (in my fifties I've begun to notice my digestion), been used to threaten small children into returning to their classrooms, and met women who assume I am in my dotage when I am simply fearful of sliding down the mountain on my bottom.

15.

Tika waits outside the hotel the next morning but, instead of heading for the bus, as I had expected, he leads me to his home. We step through a small blue door and into a courtyard, with steps leading to a rooftop and a sitting room behind us. A small shrine whiffs incense in the corner. Across some scrubby grass are rows of healthy vegetables: spinach, cauliflowers and potatoes. Tika's wife, Shobha, slim and elegant in her grey-green *salwar kameez*, offers me tea. I assume there is some hurry, but she presses me; I eat an apple, then an orange (as my bowels have coped successfully with those I ate yesterday). There are rules here but I don't know what they are. Shobha watches from the safety of a doorway.

I am more confused when we all pile into a taxi; five minutes later Shobha stops to chat to a woman I learn is her manager: she works for an agency committed to protecting young women inveigled from rural Nepal into the sex industry in India. But she is asking for the day off. She returns to the car with a grin; we will be walking together. She squashes in beside me.

'I like England; I have been there one time.'

'And I love Nepal. Everyone makes me so very welcome.'

'Would you welcome me to your house?'

'Of course I would.' She raises her eyebrows in surprise. I have known her barely half an hour and am entranced – by her gentle voice, her deep brown eyes, and by the contradictions of her shyness and her curiosity.

Our conversation stumbles on as we stroll along a gravel track to Sarangkot. She is adamant that her English is feeble, but Tika will not translate for her; she must manage on her own. We have no problems understanding each other.

It takes about an hour and a half to reach the refuge of Sarangkot; the mountains have their heads in the cloud, but we sit for our lunch with the streets of Pokhara spread across the valley far beneath us. There is whispering between Shobha and Tika; I try not to notice.

'She would like you to come to supper,' Tika tells me. 'This evening?' I feel as if I have passed some sort of test; this invitation has come from Shobha based on our discourse as we climbed the hill. I cannot begin to tell her how delighted I am to accept her invitation.

I wear my least-crumpled skirt. Shobha greets me in the doorway. She leads me up to the rooftop; a small wood fire is burning in the corner. Tika's mother, a quiet woman wrapped in shawls, peers at me with a nervous smile; she speaks no English and, on this occasion, slips away into another room. I learn that she has had long discussions with Tika; he cannot explain my travelling and I am always a mystery to her. In time we graduate to mutual smiles, but often I find her looking at me and shaking her head. No, I want to tell her, I don't know what I'm doing either.

Shobha squats by the fire and stirs pots. She leans across conspiratorially.

'It is my monthly time; I cannot go in the kitchen. There are many things in the house I cannot do. I should not be cooking for others at all; but I cook here on the roof instead.'

'Doesn't that make things difficult?'

'No – in fact it's good. I get a week off.' I can see the attraction.

Nevertheless she presents me with a delicious rice and dahl; and I am honoured with a spoon to eat it with. My efforts to eat with my fingers are embarrassingly messy. I am also pressed into the best chair; I try squatting but within a couple of minutes I topple over and Tika and Shobha are laughing unmercifully.

It grows cold as the sun sets.

Shobha cuddles herself, turns to me and asks, 'Are you lonely?'

Her directness surprises me into honesty. 'Sometimes I am lonely. And sometimes I like being able to do exactly as I please.' After weeks of a fruitless internal monologue I realise that is exactly how I feel.

'In that case you will eat here every night.'

I do. And I am grateful for it. During my stay in Pokhara the restaurant staff go on strike; they need better wages, shorter hours. Democracy is new here and needs practice. The streets are filled with shouting and red flags. 'Best stay out of their way, yes,' is Tika's advice. Only once am I trapped in an alley as they march past, in their red scarves, shouting slogans and waving flags, banging drums, thumping on the doors of every café they pass, to make sure no one is working in there. A rabble of young men, revelling in newly-recovered power. A few wave guns. I see no police.

Should I be intimidated? At the time I feel wrapped in Tika-invincibility, and am simply interested in these young men with their anger and enthusiasm.

It is only later, when the waiters in my hotel creep from their hiding places, that I acknowledge a need to be more careful. Twice I eat breakfast in my hotel in the dark; I am warned I might need to crawl under the table if the demonstrators take a close look. Apparently the image of an aging English tourist hiding under a table is not funny. One waiter is too busy acting lookout while the others shovel food at me, apparently hoping I'll swallow while it is still scalding. I oblige; their anxiety is almost infectious.

Other tourists are not so lucky. I pass them in the streets, squatting by the roadside, making a meal out of titbits from the shops and a few brave street-stalls. For three days they eat makeshift food. Local people pass them by. Hunger, they seem to say; you are trying to tell us about hunger?

It is easy for me: I have Shobha.

Tika, meanwhile, chairs the 'dialogues'.

'We will reach a solution because we must, yes. We have been too poor for too long. Now there will be investments, and health care, and education.' He crawls home at about midnight for four days running; his face is haggard and his mind still racing. He talks politics in the small hours. And he succeeds, as he had promised; cafés and restaurants re-open and owners race back into the street to urge every passing tourist to come inside.

Still Shobha nurtures me. In return I admire her vegetables; she tells me with a grin that Tika is proud of them but she does most of the work. They are rich and green; I admit my own gardening inadequacies and she insists that one day she will come to England and dig my little plot for me.

I arrive one day while she is washing clothes beneath a flowing cold tap on the rooftop.

'Your washing,' she cries. 'How do you manage your washing? Bring it here – I will do it.' I watch as her hands grow red under freezing water and insist I will do it myself, but I suspect my refusal is heard as an insult.

I am soon forgiven. 'I will be like a daughter to you. Now you have five daughters. I will come to England; and when you are old I will look after you.' It is an honour. Mothers – older mothers as I am – are treasured here. Tika's mother spends part of her time living with him, and the rest in her village in the mountains. Shobha's mother, however, is a two-day trek away. She has embraced me with all her frustrated daughterly needs and I cannot untangle what I have done to warrant such affection. Nevertheless my initial impression of a brave, intelligent, energetic and inquisitive woman is confirmed each time I meet her.

Anna, Tessa, Annie, Polly – my brave, intelligent, energetic daughters – they would love her, too.

Though I'm not so sure they would make sense of her need to look after me. We gathered when John died, found comfort together. But I needed to set an example, be a woman who made a good life for herself without a man. I worked, kept the show on the road. It was shaky at times, but I did it. Now they have young-women lives of their own; I don't want them racing home to look after me. Shobha would, willingly, dig my vegetable patch for me, tend seedlings as if they were her own; my daughters would buy me seeds and return some months later on the off-chance that anything had grown.

16.

It is the thirteenth day after Tika's uncle died. To my astonishment I am invited to the ceremony to mark the occasion; it feels an unlikely event in which to welcome a stranger. Should I wear black? (As if I carry funeral clothes around with me.) How do I say 'I'm very sorry,' in Nepali? My only protection is having grown accustomed to feeling clueless; it is less daunting these days.

Tika has been at the house since daybreak, preparing vegetables and stoking fires in the courtyard. Shobha takes me there but cannot come in; she still has her period and this excludes her from religious observances. She shrugs her farewells; I turn towards the mourning crowd, knowing Tika is in there somewhere. Although this is less alarming than my arrival at Kathmandu airport, I still feel as if I am the only person who has come to a party in fancy dress. Just as I decide to flee Tika emerges to introduce me to his aunt, a slight woman in a green sari who wrings her hands when I try to say how sorry I am. My sympathy feels clumsy; she nods anyway and I am left hoping that my mutterings make sense. Yet again I feel as if I've left the rule-book at home.

Tika leads me through the house: there are dark rooms full of women, but my place, it seems, is in the courtyard. At the far end of the yard are five wood fires; sweat drips from cooks hunched around them. Men stir huge pots of vegetables; women supervise the rice. There are heaps of dahl, sweet rolls of bread. A woman squats by the cold tap, scrubbing plates and pots, rinsing them thoroughly before they are reused. She will sit there all day, her hands raw in the stream of freezing water drawn from the mountains.

I want to lurk in a corner and watch, but am treated as a guest of honour. I must sit on the best chair, in the sunshine. An old man seems particularly concerned; we have no spoken language in common but he persists in a toothless grin, bounding up each time shade takes over my chair and returning me to the joy of sunlight. I can't work out if this is deference to my gender, ethnicity, or age. But I smile my thanks anyway.

Children gather round my knees and practise their English lessons. I draw a little puppet on my hands and we all dissolve in giggles. At least when I'm with the children I feel as if I know what I'm doing.

Tika's cousin, bare-footed and with one dusty white cloth around his waist and a second over his shoulders, comes across to talk with me. He is holding a large bowl, made from stitched chestnut leaves, full of yellow rice; he presses a blob of it on my forehead, explaining that he is giving me a blessing. I have noticed that Nepali are also given a small gift – a handkerchief, a few rupees; Tika confirms later that he has told them that I do not need a gift. I am also permitted to forego drinking the drop of water mixed with cow's urine.

'This is our culture,' Tika's cousin explains. 'I have been dressed like this for thirteen days. I can sleep on straw but I must not sit down. I cannot eat with others. But this is the last day.' He looks exhausted.

'It must be difficult. Tika has told me about it.'

'It is our culture,' he persists. 'I don't know why ...' His voice trails away.

'You must be tired.'

He nods. 'I do it for my father, I suppose.' He does not look at me.

'These are difficult days.'

He seems to gather himself and urges me to eat the food. I assure him I'll eat later – my breakfast was too recent. I thank him for making me so welcome.

'It will be interesting for you,' he says.

'Every culture has different ways of marking the days when someone dies. So yes, I am interested in what happens; but I know this must be hard for you and I am trying to think about how you feel.' I know this is clumsy, know I'm searching for the right words of comfort. He nods to acknowledge my efforts then moves away.

Later, as he passes by, he mutters. 'I don't know what I'm doing any more; I just do as the priest tells me.'

'It will soon be over.' On he wanders, an automaton with his welcome yellow rice. I remember that feeling, propelling my body through a funeral day, nodding and thanking and weeping and unable to connect with any of it. Not even the comfort, as Tika's cousin has, that I might be speeding the dead into a new incarnation. What would John say if he could see me now?

Meanwhile, the priest, in a green jumper over his long white robe, moves from room to room. I make no sense of the rituals, though it is clear that there is some sort of ceremony in each room.

Finally he gathers the close family men in a small room behind my chair; the floor is covered with leaf-dishes filled with fruit, rice-flour, a small candle and the ashy remains of a fire. The priest presents each of them with a twist of yellow thread tied around their wrists. As the cousins receive their yellow bracelets their untouchability is lifted; they can, at last, sit down.

I cannot resist the food any longer; at eleven o'clock I face a pile of rice, a cauliflower and potato curry hot enough to send me reaching for my water, sweet pickle, and a circle of fried dough – all cooked over wood fires. It is delicious; now I understand how visitors seem to be eating so much.

It is late morning when I leave. I return to the calm of the lakeside to mull over the morning. Tika is still busy with his family and Shobha is at work. I allow myself the luxury of looking back over funerals. That question – what would John say if he could see me now? It is, of course, a ridiculous question, though it hangs like a chorus through so many of my days. I like to think he would be cheering me on, but I know he would also worry about money and safety. Although eager to take risks on his own behalf he was fiercely protective of those he loved. He carried his contradictions proudly. I cling to the memories of the John that I need; the loud, energetic, generous man who believed I could take on the world.

Do I miss him; still? After twelve years? I wouldn't be asking the question if I didn't.

17.

Two days later and it is time to visit the school that Tika's father founded in his village. Tika has told me a little of his life there.

'When I was a boy there was one irrigation channel, yes, for all the fields,' he says. 'We moved a stone to direct it onto our land. We took turns. But I used to wait and, when it was dark, creep out and move the stone, so we got the water all night.' He chortles. 'Such a naughty boy, yes. And sometimes the other boys ...' His voice tails away. 'We were all naughty boys,' he says at last, with a hint of pride in his voice.

It seems there was a gaggle of them creeping round the village after dark, shifting irrigation stones and hoping to be the last to succumb to the irritated cries of their mothers.

'And now you are so well-behaved,' I say.

I can tease him now. He grins at me, shrugs as if he has no idea how that happened.

He is still busy with his dialogues on the day of the school visit, and his cousin Jeevan will walk with me. I have some books and pens; we will take them to the prize-giving. We take a taxi as far as we can, then walk along a stony river valley towards the mountains. The men are loud, animated;

Jeevan turns from time to time to make sure I am keeping up with them. I am busy gasping clean mountain air, savouring the screech of the magpie robin. It takes two puffing hours to reach Chitepani.

Celebrations have already begun. I leave goodies on the table and retreat to a bench. Immediately I am buried in children. I run the gauntlet of, 'where are you from?' and 'how old are you?'; I surrender to their inquisition without a qualm.

Meanwhile parents – almost all mothers – are intent on the game they are playing on a dusty patch of ground in front of the low school building. One is blindfolded, turned several times, then given a long stick and directed across the ground, with the aim of hitting a large ball of newspaper about ten metres away. The crowd shrieks a warning if anyone wanders too far to one side (the mountainside is steep here), and shrieks a distraction if they get close to the target. Jeevan tries to persuade me to have a turn. I shake my head, more comfortable with the children than exposed to the spotlight of a game.

At last the prize-giving begins. I ease onto a bench at the back, surrounded by women in scarlet saris. We nod and smile, share no language but I am at home among the women; we don't need a rule-book to connect with each other's dreams.

But my respite is short-lived. The woman beside me nudges me to stand; the headmaster is waving me to the front. I totter forwards, and am presented with a garland of poinsettia, marigold and sweet-smelling clover and shown to a seat among the dignitaries.

I have no idea what is going on. I find Jeevan in the crowd, mouth, 'how did this happen?' but he cannot reply for laughing. Should I shake hands with the men on each side of me? Press thanks on the headmaster? Making mistakes in the side streets of Pokhara is one thing. Here the whole village is watching. Is it offensive to speak? To say nothing? Later I will look at the photos Jeevan takes: I am wide-eyed, as if searching for answers in the camera lens.

The children stand to sing their school song – their customary adoration for the King replaced by a chant for the goddess of education. They hop from leg to leg; a small girl picks her nose; the second row sways in time to the music. I know this is part of the procedure, but for one glorious moment it feels as if they are singing for me. Brief consolation for my ignorance.

And then the speeches. It is the occasion for every local notable to talk about his or her work, the worth of each project and the progress still to be made. I wonder if there is a competition to talk for longest. The head even leans over and asks if there is anything I might like to say. As if anyone would understand me if I did. I decline – politely, I hope. (Have I got that wrong, too?) Then settle to listen, again, as the next contributor gets over-excited about something.

I try not to yawn. Stare out across the stubby playground, gaze into the mountains. Not so different from the prize-givings of my youth. I didn't listen then, either.

There is an interval for a ritual involving the education goddess. Her picture adorns the front of the table where we are sitting. I, too, am pressed to join the devotions; I manage to bow respectfully, swallowing the cough that threatens with the sting of incense. Sweat trickles down my back – it must be visible to everyone through my thin shirt. I scatter petals appropriately; lean down to accept a crimson tikka. I am expected to say something, and so mumble hopefully. I still have no idea what is going on, but someone leans across to thank me, so I must have managed well enough.

Two days later Tika shows me a newspaper article: they have written about the 'honour guest from England'! He, of course, is doubled over with laughter. But I am, indeed, honoured.

18.

After ten days I am rested. It is time to move on. Tika has agreed to introduce me to India, but first we will go to Chitwan. We say goodbye to Shobha and his daughter; I shall miss them. Tika heaves my rucksack onto the roof of the bus and we settle into our seats. We dawdle through traffic into the middle of the city and then, without warning, the bus shudders to a stop. Traffic seethes around us. Even air conditioning cannot hold back the stink of diesel from the cars and motorbikes that hem us in. Tika goes to talk to the driver: there is a strike. Local bus companies complain that tourist buses are stealing their passengers. Roads are blocked.

'Stay on the bus, yes.' Tika frowns at me, as if half-expecting me to disobey. I thought he knew me better than that. The crowd outside is thick, angry, full of men shouting and others blasting the horns on their motorbikes.

One bangs on the window. It feels like my fault. I am in the wrong place, but have no idea where the right place might be. A couple of men, Germans, I think, get off, wave their hands at the crowd and shout as if their youth and ethnicity might change anything. A young woman looks as if she might cry. A small boy behind me is copiously sick and we open the windows, but fail to evict the sour smell. I reach for my diary to scribble, describing a woman finding a pathway through the pandemonium.

It is one way of avoiding the what-if-Tika-doesn't-come-back question. It would be far worse than my butterflies (I can call them that now) at the airport in Kathmandu.

Tika, it seems, knows everyone. Eventually he returns, heavy-shouldered, and explains that he was trying to join the dialogues. But even Tika's magic does not bring peace today. The bus turns round, and heads back to the depot.

We clamber out; and then, without warning, Tika bundles me into a passing taxi with a look that says 'don't ask.' The Germans from the bus lurch towards me, shouting something about a kidnap. I try to wave them away, hoping they get the message that I leap into passing taxis every day, and hoping the police have better things to do than chase me.

The taxi heads back towards the mayhem.

'Down,' Tika tells me. I sprawl across the back seat, keeping my pale skin away from prying eyes as much as possible, and so have no warning when the driver suddenly swerves off the road and careers across a rutted field. I can sit up now. Well, after I've picked myself up from the floor.

Ten minutes ago I was marooned in a bus; now I am bouncing around in a field in a complex dance with countless taxis, buses, and brightly-painted lorries. There are no rules, no polite passing to the left. We bound across furrows and potholes; one bus lurches perilously on the small wall around a rice-paddy. Tika turns to ask if I'm fine after one particularly alarming recoil – I hit my head on the roof of the taxi – but, apart from that, he seems to treat this journey with the same equanimity as any other. I can only cling to the door handle and hope he's right. The road – when we reach it – is tame by comparison.

We make it, eventually, to the plains of Terai and village of Sauraha, close to the Royal Chitwan National Park. Fields are bigger here, sunny with mustard blooms and filled with their tangy scent. Shacks, too flimsy to survive the monsoon but manna for tourists in the dry season, dot the riverbanks. Our eventful journey is rewarded by a beer and the pink fingers of the sun setting across the water. An elephant slides along the track behind us (how do elephants tread so softly?). Monkeys chatter. Mynah birds hop close enough to see the yellow of their eyes. Such peace is incongruous after the dramas of the day.

For a few days I am a tourist. One morning I climb down to a canoe as the sun rises; the air smells of mist and the only sound is the plop of the pole punting us up the river. Even so, the guide puts his finger to his lips as we pass what seems to be a large log.

From a safe distance he says, 'Crocodile. Probably too cold for him; he is dangerous when the day is hotter. But take no chances.' We are, however, given advice on action to take if charged by a white rhinoceros: run in zigzags – their eyesight is poor and hearing you flit from side to side will confuse them. The jungle guide, proving his point, lifts his shirt to display distorting scars, the legacy of a confrontation with a rhino. If it's that dangerous, what am I doing here? I ran out of courage in Manly. We tiptoe, obediently; rhinoceros keep to a safe distance today. But there are prints from tiger paws on the sand beside the river.

'Last night, I think,' we are told. 'But if tiger come – dead. Cannot kill tiger. Protected.' Maybe the tiger would prefer to eat the young, I tell myself; surely I'm a bit gristly.

The next morning I cannot resist an early walk to listen to the birds, along with a Finnish couple from the resort. We hear many more than we see; the damp morning air is alive with every twitter and chat of the jungle. I want only to sit in a corner and listen. But the guide is responsible for my safety; I follow, obediently.

There is more shushing: the guide has spotted a wild boar, grunting and snuffling, about five metres away, through the trees. The Finnish man inches forward with his camera; I follow from what seems a respectful distance.

And then – without warning – the boar charges at us. This is not the time to reach for the diary and think how interesting this is. Instead – the scattering of tourists. A cacophony of crashing; the snapping of crumpled vegetation. No time to notice thorns as I hurtle through shrubs. As the oldest by far, my progress must be slower than the others; tiger, wild boar – they might prefer the succulent young but I would be much easier pickings. I smash through bushes – then am suddenly aware of silence behind me. Such a contrast to my pounding heart and puffing lungs.

One by one tourists emerge, foliage dangling from hair and sundry animal poo clinging to their shoes, from the jungle. Blood trickles down my leg from thorn assaults. The guide seems rooted to the spot. He is laughing too hard to speak.

'Here – see – his sows. He want just to reach his sows. You were in the way; that is all.'

There is a titter of embarrassed giggles; the man swaggers a little; the woman and I stay close to each other waiting for our hearts to resume a more reliable pace. She looks across at me, as if she expects me to act my age and reassure her, while I am trying to tame my own panic.

By the time we return most of us can laugh at ourselves, though suddenly, I'm not so sure about spotting a tiger in the wild. I think, with momentary sorrow, of my Wiltshire sheep; they might be silly but at least they won't eat me.

The year turns. It is New Year's Eve. I have been invited to a 'cultural programme' at my resort. It is a cold night. We – a group of Danes, Nepali and Indians – gather round a bonfire and wait for the display team to arrive.

We are chilled through by the time they make it. But the gentle rhythms of Tharu music excite me, and their use of sticks and percussion remind me both of English morris dancing and Maori celebrations in New Zealand. I need no second invitation when a dancer waves me to join the end of the line. I catch a glimpse of Tika, laughing – of course – but I don't care. I shake the bells I am given, wave my hands and stamp my feet hopefully, wallow in the firelight and the chattering of the jungle and the music.

In the darkness I forget my middle-aged self-consciousness and allow the music to take over.

The Indians, too, need little encouragement to join in. A woman in a blue sari, orange cardigan and pink woollen gloves seizes me by the hand and urges me into the melee of her large family. We surge round and round the fire, hot now, faces scorched in the heat and backs sweating in sympathy.

There is a smell of night, woodsmoke, whiffs of incense. Feet tap faster and faster; still my hand is held by a woollen glove as we weave onwards, and onwards.

A pause. I am gasping for breath. The woman's family gather round me, ask if I will stand in their photographs. They are, I learn, from Mumbai; staying here on holiday. We exchange rudimentary information; they are curious about my trip.

'But why are you travelling?' I am unprepared for the starkness of the question, and fumble my reply.

'There must be a reason. For learning?' That will do for now.

Later, when the fire has died down and we have retreated to bed, I ponder the question again. In the comfort of my kitchen I decided to travel to see if I could do this, without really knowing what "this" is. Tonight it was dancing round a fire holding the gloved hand of an Indian woman.

And tomorrow – who knows? But maybe that's the point – the unknown shape of all those tomorrows. But I am beginning to love travelling simply because I can.

Well, with Tika I can. He has quietly supervised a transition from terrified ignorance to almost-comfortable cluelessness. In calm moments I flick though my *Lonely Planet* for India. Although Tika will be with me for a couple of weeks, I will spend three months in India, alone.

I'm not sure I'm ready for alone.

19.

It is two kilometres from our hotel in Bhairahawa to the Indian border. The gentle warmth of Chitwan is behind us. It is bitterly cold: I am wearing both trousers and skirt, have four layers of t-shirts, fleeces, hat, gloves and a blanket. I must look like my grandmother in winter. Our rickshaw driver wears a stringy *lungi*, a woollen jumper that is in the process of unravelling, and plastic sandals.

Nobody would have noticed if we had simply cycled through the border. Nepalis and Indians cross freely; had Tika and the driver not steered me through the shambles of lorries and stalls and people to the immigration offices I suspect I would have entered India unaware of the lack of stamps on my passport. The Nepalis shelter in a dark room smelling of curry with a splintered desk and map of the world on the wall and seem disappointed I am leaving their country; the Indians perch behind a table at the side of the road. There are no computers, no security check.

We have four hours on a bus to Gorakhpur. Slowly, so slowly, the fog lifts to reveal the northern plains. Fields are bigger here than in Nepal, and – from what we see here – fertile. There are acres of rice, wheat, mustard, banana and sugar cane. And there are pockets of industry, brickworks and cement processing, both swamped by clouds of dust and gravel heaps. I spot a sign by the side of the road with an explicit picture urging people to defecate in toilets and not in the fields. And an advertisement for vests.

We arrive in Gorakhpur in the late morning, and I am hurtled into the pandemonium of India. Tika rushes to retrieve our luggage from the top of the bus before a porter seizes it and tries to steer us to his chosen hotel. The survival of my tinsel is bleak consolation for this mayhem. *Tuk tuk* drivers press around me. I cannot believe the crowds; Kathmandu was busy, but this is commotion. Tika, of course, is phlegmatic, strides off towards our hotel, carving his own path through the masses. I follow, meekly. The only alternative is to give in to terror.

I cling to his side as we negotiate our way beside a row of street cafés; the air is thick with the smells of cheap frying oil and curry and roasting nuts and diesel – and cows. Mangy dogs lurk in corners. Chickens scratch among the heaps of rubbish. An onslaught of noise – hoots from taxis and *tuk tuks*, revving engines, yells from men on the grubby stalls, the grumble of a train in the station opposite. Just when I had begun to understand travelling, India assaults me. I long, briefly, for the silent hills of Wiltshire. There is no space for thinking here.

We have been warned that our hotel is 'basic.' It is. The floor is a cracked and grimy marble, the walls may once have been a delicate green but are now streaked with brown finger marks (I don't ask). I have a brown curtain, but it covers less than half the window – which will not close. The toilet does not flush. There is a scuttle of cockroaches.

We are opposite the station – convenient for our early train tomorrow. I watch as a man pumps water into a bucket by the roadside; beside him another man pees into the gutter. It takes effort to resist words like 'horrified'; all those glorious photographs of India's colours and the reality is this. Where are the ashrams, the yogis, the sunsets? I have three months in India; whatever made me think that was a good idea?

Tika has been here before. He ignores the mayhem. I envy the core of him that can keep calm. He takes no notice of my alarms.

'It is just India,' he says. And laughs. I think I'd disintegrate if he didn't laugh.

An early night. Surely I'll feel better after some sleep. I try ear-plugs to keep out the din. They fail. Clamour from the stalls and *tuk tuk* drivers fades in the small hours, replaced by thunderous chanting from the station tannoy: 'Hare Krishna, Rama Rama'. Three o'clock, four o'clock – on and on it goes. I know it is a sacred chant but right now it feels a spiritual as a football song. And as persistent. I can only assume it is designed to deter the hordes sleeping in the station. It fails; bodies are stretched across every inch of floor space when we gather on the platform in the morning. I step across wet trails in the platform; four people are cleaning their teeth at a fountain with a notice announcing it is drinking water. I am only surprised that it doesn't smell worse.

My hotel had held its secret until the moment before I left. When I turned to check I'd left nothing, I found, scribbled on the wall above the bedhead, the words, 'I love you.' I grin; romance can flourish in unlikely places. I remember romance.

20.

The platform at Varanasi is shorter than the train. Tika leaps down to the track with his customary agility; I stand at the top and peer at a six-foot drop. I might have been able to bound down when I was twenty, but not now. I need to turn round and negotiate my descent backwards. But I cannot turn round in the narrow passage with my rucksack, plus its incongruous tinsel, on my back. I reverse, manage a three-point turn in the corner, then inch backwards to the doorway. By this time Tika is doubled over with laughter, quite unable to help as I launch myself out of the train, hoping for footholds, and praying my skirt will protect my modesty. By the time my feet crunch on the gravel beside the tracks I, too, am giggling helplessly. This is one of the most sacred Hindu cities, and we have both fallen at its feet.

It is not a graceful way to honour Varanasi. It claims to be the oldest living city, with continuous settlement dating back to the eighth century BC (Damascus makes similar assertions; and archaeologists are unconvinced). Legend has it that the city was founded by the Hindu god, Lord Shiva. It boasts an ancient university where students wallow in Sanskrit texts, and sanctified *ghats* spread along the banks of the sacred river Ganges. Neither Mogul invasions nor British occupation have diluted Hindu reverence for the city and its river.

We drop our luggage at a hotel and are about to leave to explore the *ghats* when one of the men behind the reception desk calls us back.

'Be careful,' he warns. 'You must not know each other. If

police come you must say that Tika is your friend. There are problems with mixed couples, drugs; the police may suspect you.' He will not be more specific, but repeats the warning several times, making sure we understand. I do not know how to suggest that no one could possibly mistake us for a couple when I am old enough to be Tika's mother. But Tika nods his understanding; not everything is as peaceful as it seems in Varanasi.

We thread our way past stalls laden with cricket bats, mobile phones, roasting sweetcorn (oh, that smell), betel nuts. Traffic – buses, taxis, clean cars with chauffeurs in polite hats, rattling cars without doors, rickshaws, autos – all compete for every available square metre of road space. There is the roar of engine noise and reek of diesel fumes. And dust; there is a collective coughing and ritual spitting from the dust. *Tuk tuk* drivers hover beside us; beggars pull at my sleeve.

Where are the women? These streets are populated almost entirely by men. My shoulders are covered and my skirt reaches to mid-calf, but men stare at me. Everything about me stands out: my ethnicity, my gender, my age. The antithesis of the invisibility I expect at home, that hid me in New Zealand. I try to take no notice.

On into the Old City; here the streets are far too narrow for cars. We thread a path through wizened men in ragged *lungis*, chanting *sadhus*, grubby children, cows, water buffalo, dogs, goats, wagons laden with vegetables or dead chickens, stalls heaped with bright bags and scarves and joss sticks, offers of samosas and sweets and *paan* – somehow they fit together like jigsaw pieces in these narrow passageways. The singing of sitars creeps through open doorways; incense seeps through cracks in walls; there are invitations to learn yoga/music/meditation on every corner. Overwhelmed by the sensory bombardment I slip in cow-poo, retch from the corner-stinks of pee – and begin to feel inaugurated into the realities of India.

I am walking a respectful distance behind Tika when three

suited men slide between us. He strides purposefully on; I stride purposefully after him. There are glances between the men but I will not look at them; they seem to be trying to edge me away from Tika's path but I skate around them and continue on my way. They melt into the crowd; Tika turns, nods at me, and we carry on. A hundred yards further on and we are aware of being followed. We repeat our ignoring procedure and again he slips away.

'Did you see them?' I ask Tika later.

'Of course.'

'But what ....'

'We will not think about what they wanted, what could have happened.' The tone of his voice makes it clear that he will not entertain fantasies about possible dangers. I have not been whisked into a back street to be robbed of my few worldly goods, nor beaten and abandoned by the riverside. He will not even allow me a second or two of smug panic.

Even without such lurking dangers, the pandemonium of these streets baffles me. I veer from wanting to explore every alleyway, creep into every temple, inhale every whiff of incense, to recoiling from this bombardment and hide in the safety of the hotel. Without Tika I have no doubt I would resort to the hiding option.

This is no preparation for the shocking mysteries of the Ganges. We emerge at the top of a flight of steps and drop down to the *ghats* and the glories of the river. Those who bathe here have their sins washed away. Those who die here and have their ashes scattered in the river are promised the easiest pathway to their next incarnation.

The setting sun filters an orange glow across the water. Ancient buildings, built from red or yellow sandstone, echo the blush of the river. There is city noise – and there is a strange hush. I am faced with a spirituality that I cannot define, but which is almost tangible enough to hold.

Old men in white *lungis* wander along the *ghats*, then sink into the water with a sigh. Groups of young men plunge into the river together: religious observance can be fun. And there are women here, immersing themselves in the water and then spreading metres of bright saris across the *ghats* to dry: a dazzling patchwork of saris in the evening light. A child offers me a candle, another garlands of marigolds. Beggars slump on steps, hold out pathetic hands. *Sadhus*, with their rich orange robes and sacred painted faces, sit in meditative splendour. The air is thick with dust, with the putrid smell of the water, with incense, with spices from the samosa stalls.

Scrawny dogs sniff heaps of rubbish; one has running sores, others heave by with sagging teats. Water buffalo gather on uneven steps. A goat is giving birth in a corner. We pass a fallen cow; it seems she has slipped on the steps and is unable to get up. Two days later she is still there; someone has put a cushion beneath her head and a rough cloth across her middle; her eyelids flicker and her breathing is erratic. I have to swallow western sensibilities about animal suffering. Life and death is in the hands of the Gods in India.

We pause by the burning *ghats*. We are not alone; it is common for local people as well as tourists to gather to watch this ritual. Bodies, swathed in glorious red and gold, are carried to the river, sprinkled with water and then unwrapped and eased into the piles of wood and burnt. There are no keening women, just the quiet tears of men.

As we watch, a solitary man passes by us with the swaddled body of a baby; he makes his way to the water's edge, holds the child to his breast and then slips it gently into the water. Mother Ganga will care for it now. He turns, melts back into the crowd. I want to weep for him.

We revisit the Ganges at dawn. It is what tourists do. We bob down the river in a little boat, with a thousand tiny candles twinkling in the blue dawn light. Steps and temples and water melt into the early sky. The river – black and putrid – is alive with morning swimmers. It is too early for the sun to begin to warm the river's stink.

A small boy clambers from boat to boat, selling tiny candles.

'Say a prayer to Mother Ganga, then give the candle to the river,' he tells us. Nobody barters.

I buy my candle, rest it gently on the water, watch as it bobs hopefully in a sea of tiny candles. And try to stifle tears. Under my breath I ask the river, this river that is the giver and taker of life in India, to look after my baby. My new grandson.

Three weeks before I left, Tessa told me she was pregnant. Her current plan is to have the baby in Venezuela. There was no time before I set off to begin to engage with the meaning of grandparenthood. I know it's a rite of passage that many women look forward to; but I wasn't ready for it. Not yet. I had travelling to do.

But now from across the other side of the world, I gaze at pictures of her scan, the tiny fingers, the huge forehead. It will be a boy; already she has given him a name. In the pink morning light of Varanasi, with the Ganges slapping against the side of the boat and my little candle bobbing its way to the sea, I know that I will love him, too. It is a loving that makes me cry.

Suddenly the boat tilts as Tika lurches to his feet, dips his hand in the river and sprinkles water on his head. My tears dry as quickly as they began.

'It is my holy thing,' he explains. 'Now I am free from sin. So I can have a beer tonight.' He bursts into his glorious grin.

21.

It is time to leave Varanasi. Tika and I gather our bags and hail a *tuk tuk*. Our driver weaves a silent path through the diesel fumes.

The station, of course, is overflowing. We clamber down; Tika seizes his case and the driver helps to haul my rucksack onto my back. I pay him without thinking and turn away.

'Take care!' our driver calls after me. I swing round, catch his dark eyes for just a second, and he disappears into the throng. Where did he learn to say that? Where did his compassion grow from? Has he any idea of the impact his sudden words of kindness have on me? I have been stared at, pointed to, followed, made to feel like an exhibit. And this man, a ragged man with nothing to his name but a *tuk tuk*, makes a point of responding to me as a woman.

Again I want to cry. I seem to be doing a lot of crying these days. But the mayhem of the station at Varanasi is not the place for a therapeutic blub.

Tika and I have just five more days together. We plan a trip into the mountains: I want to go looking for tigers (from the safety of a Landrover). We make it as far as Lucknow, where I am felled by a dodgy spring roll. I crawl from the comfort of my bed to the grim toilet and back. I sleep for hours, my waking moments filled with nothing more exciting than another trip to the toilet, the rhythm of a dripping tap, and – from somewhere beyond this sanctuary – a Muslim call to prayer.

Tika tells me later that he spends the time walking the streets of Lucknow looking for a doctor, and wondering if he should override my protestations and seek medical advice. He returns every couple of hours, knocking on my door before the invasion of the hall-light disrupts the dark solace of my sickroom.

In the evening he eats his supper sitting on my bed.

'Please, a little boiled rice, yes,' he says. His voice is tired. I am anything but hungry, but I manage a little, to keep him happy. And it stays in situ long enough to satisfy him.

It is twenty-four hours before I can stand long enough to shower. Two days before I make it down to breakfast.

'I'll have an omelette,' I decide. Tika raises his eyebrows but says nothing. My omelette, when it arrives, looks innocuous. I glance up from the shock of my first mouthful to see Tika giggling.

'You want no chilli, you must ask, yes,' he says. The roof of my mouth is on fire. I must be better.

We have no time, now, for tiger-hunting in the mountains. We make do with convalescence in Lucknow. Tika will not admit to being bored, though I know he is.

On our final day we take a taxi to the Memorial Park. I revel in relief from the streets, the surprise of green grass. We are paused beside a concrete sculpture that I do not understand when a man waves us over. He sits with his back to a tree; his fingers play with a gun and my eyes stray to the array of bullets on the ground in front of him. I am not good with guns; even the toy variety makes me queasy; this is a grown-up gun with a trigger. And bullets.

'Where are you from?' the man asks. 'And where is your supporter?' I gather he means husband, or at least chaperone. He strokes his gun, pats the ground beside him with a clear invitation to sit down. He gives me that wink, the wink my brother used to practise when he was sixteen, the wink that means, 'how about it'. Does he want to marry me? Make me his concubine?

My palms are sweating. This is not the time for explanations.

'My husband is in Chennai,' I explain. 'He is working, and I am exploring the north. Tika is my friend.' Tika chortles beside me; I will not look at him. Rather I persist in this lie, describe how I telephone my husband every night, how he has the ear of the highest politician, the most important policemen. The man still pats the grass, plays with his gun. Winks. My voice begins to squeak. I invent the most prestigious, fiercest, possessive husband I can imagine. Still he winks. And strokes his gun. My stomach turns to water.

Tika quietly steers me away from him. He, of course, is giggling. It takes four hours for me to think my exaggerated fibbing might be funny.

'You have learned,' he tells me later. 'Not always the truth here, yes.'

New Delhi. Tika's flight is booked, and a friend is to join me for a couple of weeks. We sit over our final meal and muse on our weeks together.

Our initial contract – for him to guide me through the hills of Nepal and introduce me to the complexities of India – has disappeared beneath a deeper connection.

When I emerged into the glare of Kathmandu he chuckled at my unease and led me gently into whirling streets. He was my shepherd in the mountains of Nepal, my escort in the chaotic streets of India. My urge to hide from the pandemonium around me has subsided. Curiosity has taken over from alarm; I can cross the road, buy a bus ticket and negotiate the trains; I can ask questions.

This has, of course, been a journey for two of us. But the change, it feels, has been mine rather than his. His humour – gently mocking – has never let us down. He has quietly supervised my health and my safety without me feeling overlooked or mollycoddled, and now I can step off on my own.

At least I think I can.

He is a witty, humble, generous man. I will miss him.

We part on the steps of a hotel. I close my hands in a Nepali *namaste*; he responds with a brief western hug and a whispered, 'Take care'. We are both aware of the Varanasi echo.

Of course I retreat to my hotel room and cry. For the baby, for the *tuk tuk* driver, for the loss of Tika. For the quiet Wiltshire countryside, almost three months away now. For my daughters. Even their tinsel fails to cheer me.

But I am too far from home for grieving. Misery, sometimes, is a choice – one I cannot indulge here for long. If I am to survive here I must at least look as if I'm capable, know what

I'm doing, and not some wilting woman who dissolves into tears when the going gets rough. I splash my face, rearrange what I hope looks like a smile, and go out to search for a cup of tea. It is a middle-aged solution, and it works.

PART FOUR

I AM A DREADFUL MEMSAHIB

22.

Pip, a friend from home, is flying to meet me in Delhi. We have travelled together before, understand each other's ways, know that we both faff at bedtime and are best left alone. We had mused on finding our own way around – I believe I can do that now – but she has just two weeks holiday. Given the challenges of travelling in India we settle for a group holiday as the only way to see anything and have time together.

She arrives at New Delhi airport – the old airport – at two in the morning. I have my pyjamas on under my skirt, having grabbed a couple of hours sleep before coming out. I can't manage two in the morning these days without a bit of a kip, as my father would have said.

She is one of the last passengers to arrive, and we cling to each other as if it were years since we last met. She is grey with tiredness; she complains that her mouth tastes of planes and coffee; and I bounce around her like a puppy. I want her to smell of home, of Wiltshire, of winter, of jacket potatoes and cheese. She doesn't, of course, but I can pretend. Any whiff of homesickness disappears while she is here.

The tour group gallops round New Delhi, Agra, and Rajasthan.

At first we can enthuse about the magnificence of

Humayun's Tomb, wonder at the phallic power of the Red Fort and Qutb Minar. On to Agra. The Taj Mahal sinks into a pale blue as the sun sets; at dawn the marble is a silver grey against the lightening sky, gradually turning blue, then purple, red, orange, and yellow before finally wearing its daytime white. We shuffle with crowds smelling of feet past the tomb smothered in jewels.

But there is no time to linger. We must visit the abandoned city of Fatehpur Sikri, with its three palaces for three queens, as well as a multi-storey construction for concubines. On we rush, to the Keoladeo National Park, where a little bird is singing 'Kapil Dev, Kapil Dev'; cricket infects even the birds in India.

One hour later, and we are driving in the dust of Rajasthan. We speed past the pink walls of Jaipur, leap out to take a photograph of the Hawa Mahal; then on to the Amber Palace. We stop at the Jantar Mantar, hurtle off to Jaipur's City Palace, then on to Jodhpur, and the Mehrangarh, a palace built on the hilltop within the city walls. We gawp at more intricacies; there are no peaceful corners.

Four days respite in a dusty village; but no time for resting. We must walk! Stride up the hillside to a temple; hike beside the lake. Quick, there is just time to visit another Jain temple, then off to Udaipur, to admire the palace where *Octopussy* was filmed. Pip and I feel an urge to sing the James Bond theme, but the others simply look at us. Maybe they are too tired to join in.

We land, eventually, in Mumbai. In spite of the racing we have savoured our time together. I suspect we have not been ideal group members. We know we should be interested as our guide wades through the mysteries of Indian history and religion, but behave more like schoolgirls at the back of the class. We can always read it up later, we agree. For us, this two weeks is about being together, discovering what we can for ourselves (the few occasions when we had time away from the group were the most precious); reflections on the lessons of India will have to wait.

She has also seen Anna, collected birthday presents (including the knickers from Tessa). She is an umbilical link; I didn't realise how much I needed that until she came.

The group prepares to disband. Holidays, I realise, are a disruption to the normal scheme of things, while travelling is a way of being in itself – not an escape from, but a discovery in its own right. The pursuit of pleasure is, of course, part of the package; but so is standing in queues for three hours trying to get a train ticket; so is trying to find somewhere to buy toothpaste; so is retreating to one's room, bored, in the evening hours when the streets are too full of men to feel safe. Holidays whisk you away, and whisk you home again. Travelling leaves you with the questions, the discomforts, and the glorious curiosity that sends you on to the next town, the next temple, the next beach. With a year to myself I have permission to stand and stare, to tease out a view of myself in the worlds around me, to take the risk of empathy amid the unfamiliar and untried.

We have had two weeks together and Pip must go home. She takes part of me with her.

I spend the afternoon by a pool. There is enough breeze to flutter on my arms and wave the leaves of pot plants smothering the balcony. There are car hoots, and crows; somewhere a pneumatic drill is breaking up a road – taking work from men and women with pickaxes. But my sadness is not hollow. I feel I need to suspend reflections for a while, to notice without trying to understand, to reach into unthinking places where sights and sounds and smells and even, possibly, religion, finds its own logic. It is like unravelling knitting; I hope it will take a recognisable shape eventually.

Most of all, I have to adjust to being truly alone. There are no more plans for anyone to join me, no more guides waiting to steer me through. From now on it's just me and the diary.

23.

The cousin of a colleague from work lives in Mumbai; he has agreed to help me plan my journey south. I assume that we will simply meet, discuss an idea or two over my *Lonely Planet*, and I'll be on my way. He has other ideas.

Vedesh is a thickset, solid man in his forties, and taller than many Indians. He launches into a running commentary as our taxi weaves through the nowfamiliar chaos.

'You will find things very different here. You need to understand that. The caste system is very old; it has been here forever; the politicians think they can reform it but they cannot. The poor are happy; it is best to leave them as they are. The slums are squalid, but they are happy there. The government should not interfere.'

'I have tried not to use the word squalid; it sounds so ... so judgmental.' I manage to interrupt him.

'Not at all. What other word can describe them? And do not give money to the children; they are sent begging by parents who spend all the money on drink. Parents are having children just to send them out begging. And many beggars are rich; you must not give to them. It is different where I live.' I can't quite follow the non-sequitur but it obviously makes sense to him.

'I live with my parents – we are Brahmin actually – but I was brought up by my aunt; my father went to England to work and my mother went with him. I had twin sisters and she took one with her, and left me and my other sister with my aunt. But my sister – the one with me, she died. And my uncle – he's a cook, that's what Brahmin's are, cooks, actually (I had thought that Brahmin were priests? Later I confirm that many are, indeed, cooks.) – he was away most of the time. I left home, spent most of my childhood in hostels, and with the street children. Now I live with my parents.' I'm not sure I'm following all this.

'But soon, next month, I will go to Kerala, to the temple.

There is a festival; I must grow a beard, and cannot drink alcohol, and if I were married I must be celibate.' He is beginning to remind me of Victor and his diatribes in Rotorua. Have I really travelled all this way only to find Walter Mitties?

'My sister, she lives in Kent, in England. She has adopted a child from an orphanage in Chennai. I found the child for her (he shows me a photograph); she loves me, this little girl. She is happy in England now, but when we first found her she loved me more than my sister. You see, I organised the adoption actually, and I visited her every month; it took a whole year before all the papers were signed and my sister could come to collect her.'

There is no pause in the monologue, and so I bring out photographs of my daughters, hoping that maybe this can begin to look more like a conversation.

'And they are married?'

'Three are married, and one has a long-term boyfriend; I think she will be married soon,' I lied. Indians cannot conceive of leaving unmarried daughters to make their own decisions; and Lucknow taught me lying.

'What are their names?' Vedesh rounds on me with the question. Two of my daughters are stepchildren; there has never been a problem with an Annie and an Anna, but suddenly I know I cannot explain this. My mind races over names.

'This is Anna, and this Tessa, and this is Polly – she's the one who isn't married – and this (oh help) is Janet!' Janet! JANET!! Where did that come from? What will she say when she knows I have renamed her Janet? All those months, years, building a relationship with her and I drop another name on her without a by-your-leave. I am, indeed, a terrible stepmother. (Within hours I am able to ring her; she cannot reply for giggling. Not such a wicked stepmother, then.) Vedesh takes no notice.

'Polly, she is beautiful. I think I am a little in love with

Polly. You must check out her boyfriend; he must be right for her. You should be very careful.' He lingers over her photograph. I have no doubt that Polly would eat him for breakfast. I fall out of the taxi with relief when we reach his club.

I have an afternoon to recover; we must meet for supper. We pass a friend on our way out and he introduces me:
'This is Dr Joan; she is a professor, actually, my sister's professor.' I have a PhD, awarded on completion of a research study in play therapies. I am not a professor. But I cannot interrupt Vedesh in front of his friend.
I tackle him later. 'I am not a professor; that isn't true.'
'But you are a doctor, and that is a professor.'
'No, it isn't; and more than that I am not your sister's professor.'
'Sister, cousin – it is all the same here. And you supervise my cousin.'
'Well, no. We work together.'
'But you are senior to her.'
'No, we work together.'
'But you have been working longer than she has; sometimes you show her what to do; and so you are senior.'
'It doesn't work like that. I have been working longer, but we are colleagues, we are the same.'
'You are senior, professor – it is the same.'
'No. We are colleagues; we learn from each other.'
'You are a good Hindu. Humility is a Hindu virtue; in another life you were a Hindu.'
I give up.

We take a *tuk tuk* to his parents' flat. We alight by a small courtyard, to climb concrete steps. Vedesh's mother greets me with an unexpected hug. His father, over eighty, shrivelled and very dark-skinned, in pale *lungi* and whitish shirt, sits in the corner and gives up on conversation; I try to talk to him and Vedesh moves in to translate, but his father seems to melt into the wall.

His mother brings me tea, puts her chair conspiratorially close to mine; this is a conversation for women.

'The Gods have blessed you with lovely daughters,' she tells me. Indeed they have. 'I had two daughters, and one died. My husband, he had to work in England; my mother, she say I must leave one child with her; it was my duty. I have no choice. And my mother, she say I must leave Vedesh; he was a little boy and I cannot forgive myself for leaving him. And look at me now.'

I look at her; she is a small, shrewd-eyed woman with the odd missing tooth and glasses.

'My husband never thanks me for anything; I get up at four o'clock every morning to give him coffee before he goes to the temple (she is sitting with her back to him, indicating the subject under discussion with an occasional wave of her hand); he is in the temple for hours and I am alone. Vedesh tries to work; he had work, with a British firm, but was made redundant eight years ago. Now there is no work. He is a good man. He has no money. My daughter was getting older and we worried, so Vedesh found her a husband, used all his savings for the wedding, and now she is happy. He should be married; I cannot forgive myself for leaving him. I can only do my duty.'

It is the outpouring of an unheard woman. I cannot begin to comment on her world of ungrateful men, worries about adult children. It is certainly a conversation I've enjoyed (I use the word deliberately) with friends in numerous coffee shops. The chit-chat of sunny mornings. But her words have a different, desperate, quality – as if she has no one else who might hear her. All I can do is listen from the comfort of the 'best chair': a cane chair with a cushion; I nod and smile, and hold her wrinkled hand.

She sits on a grimy plastic chair; behind her is a bed frame with a couple of thin mattresses, covered with a faded pink cloth; one wall is full of undusted shelves with a TV, a holy picture and family photographs. She finds me looking across at them.

'That is my daughter and her family. When they came to see us she wore a western dress, with her knees and the tops of her arms showing. He (she nods behind me) was furious, but could do nothing.' I wonder, briefly, what he would have made of my daughters, at sixteen, ready to go clubbing; all I could do was insist I would pick them up at midnight and hope they would not be too cold.

Vedesh emerges from the shower; we must leave, he insists, he has to take me back to the club and then go to a wedding. His mother clings; I can find no way to comfort her. I want to respond as a daughter, as I did when my mother was old and frail, to buy her books and make her cups of tea and take her out for a drive to look at the snowdrops in spring, to listen while she told the stories of her girlhood in the thirties.

In the *tuk tuk* Vedesh announces that he will join me for supper; it is my birthday, he cannot let me celebrate alone. And, in spite of the restrictions placed on him before his pilgrimage, he will have a drink with me, providing I tell no one. He downs four whiskies and I stop listening.

We decide to plan my journey the next morning. Vedesh marches me to a travel agent and introduces me as professor from Oxford. It is not a good beginning. I clutch my *Lonely Planet*; I have ideas, I tell them; I do not need luxury but do need to be safe.

The agent makes countless phone calls; he sighs, then scowls; Vedesh talks endlessly in Hindi; finally I am presented with a plan – flights, hotels, a car in Kerala, and a huge invoice. I query why I need to fly; the stations are too dangerous at night, they insist. I query the car in Kerala; the buses are too dangerous, they drive off the road, they insist. The hotels – I do not need smart hotels? It is difficult to find hotels; there is a festival, all hotels are full. I can either walk out and begin alone, or accept, in spite of what I know to be an exorbitant price. I take the easy option. At least it means I can fly out of Mumbai in the morning.

For two days I have drowned in words. At times Vedesh's grandiosity irritated me; but then I remember: he has been unable to find work for eight years, in a country where status is defined by work and caste.

We say affectionate farewells, and he sends his love to Polly.

24.

It is five weeks since the shock of Gorakhpur; I have overdosed on the stimuli of India. Ten days in Goa: just what I need.

The agent in Mumbai has found me a hotel that has been open for less than a week; builders collect around a pit that will one day be a pool and all meals are in our rooms as the restaurant is still a pile of bricks. Before I left home I might have complained; now – this is India. At least I have somewhere to sleep.

I linger on my balcony each morning while the street awakes. The terracotta earth has an orange hue in the early light; the smell of the rubbish heap across the road does not reach me here. A woman sprinkles water in front of the hotel, in an effort to control the dust. Crows screech; there is the twitter of something smaller; a black hen and two chicks scratch in the dirt beside the road. Crockery clatters downstairs. Someone is washing in the trees across the road, half-hidden by a makeshift screen.

There is a trail of stalls between the hotel and middle of town; around here they are run by women and children; men govern the richer pickings in the town centre. But every stallholder has the same cry:

'Come, look; look is free. I give you good price.'

Every rupee is precious; I am an unrewarding tourist; I have no space for extra trinkets. That does not stop me feeling guilty as I stride past stall after stall knowing that even a few rupees can make a difference.

'I have no space,' I try to explain.

To which one woman responds with a rant, in her own language, a screaming which follows me down the street, presumably along the lines of 'you arrogant tourist making feeble excuses not to come into my shop'. Dark eyes follow me. With neither the language, nor the courage, to return and face her, I can only walk away and hope she is simply having a bad day.

But I cannot ignore the little girl who runs the stall beneath my balcony. She is slight, dark-skinned and sharp-eyed, a small eagle of a child; she has two dresses: one is long and green, and probably fitted her a year ago, and the second is pink satin, and will probably fit her next year. She has no shoes.

She tells me her name is Lolita; and she is nine years old. I watch as she opens her stall at eight o'clock every morning, stretching with a pole three times taller than she is to slip a tarpaulin from its moorings and expose her assortment of merchandise. Then she heaves bricks across the dust before asking a neighbour to help her with a tabletop of necklaces, before pulling racks of shirts and skirts from their nightly hiding-place. The process is reversed at around eleven o'clock at night.

When she thinks no one is looking she skips down the street.

I stop to chat with her every morning on my way to the beach.

'I speak English,' she tells me, 'and so I work here. I have a big sister, but she no English; and my parents no English. I went to school, but not any more; now I work here. My little brother, he is six, he go to school.'

She presses my rescue buttons; it seems unjust that – the brightest in her family – she should be denied education. I want to explore the cost of lessons, though I know I won't; and rightly so – without her income the family would starve. Reading and writing are luxuries. I should know that. When I was young, educating women was seen as a luxury, not worth the money when all we would do was get married and have babies. I wasn't popular, wanting to stay on at school after 'O' levels, to go to university. Not surprising, I suppose, that one of my daughters asked if I remembered the Romans.

Lolita has a baby sister; a woman sits and rocks a feebly-crying child, stroking her head and stooping to kiss her dark curls from time to time. At night, when it is quiet, I can hear this crying from the sanctuary of my room. After twenty-four hours I make my way to the stall; surely they will accept help with doctor's fees and antibiotics.

But Lolita explains, 'My mother, she has gone back to the village. The baby, she is sick. Maybe an uncle will come to help me. But the baby ...' Three days later her mother returns, without the baby.

Again, it is Lolita who completes the story. 'No money for medicines, not for girl.' She launches at a passing tourist before I can find words of comfort. Besides, I have no way of knowing what this death means to this Hindu family. I only know what it would mean to me. That's where I run out of words.

I peer from my balcony one evening to watch as Lolita sidles up to two men on their way back from town. Once she has their attention she will not let them go, showing them shirt after bag after trinket. I raise a silent cheer as they walk away with two necklaces; the next morning I congratulate her on the sale.

'They were from England,' she tells me. 'They say they have no money, will bring me three hundred rupees today. I will look for them.'

I watch as she scans passing faces all day. Her Englishmen never return. It is all she had sold that day. I buy an overpriced shirt; it is the best I can do.

25.

There is respite on the beach. It is the wedding season: honeymoon couples drift along the sands, hand-in-hand; eyes only for each other. I hope I'll never be too old to remember that feeling. The urgency of touching; the astonishment that being with this man makes everything in the world feel wonderful.

Many Indian marriages are arranged; I have read the 'matrimonials' section in the newspaper, placed by families looking for partners for their sons and daughters. I have seen wedding parties in Rajasthan: noisy, glittering revelries that weave their way through the streets. But these young people, shyly doe-eyed with each other, appear to be as enraptured as lovers all over the world. They make me smile, just to watch them.

I muse on their happiness on the bus to Panjim. A pale, skinny Englishwoman, her lime green top exposing freckled shoulders and scrawny neck slides onto the seat beside me. We stare, silent companions, out of the window until an Indian woman squeezes in beside her. Then she raises her eyes, as if to complain at the need for such proximity to a local woman. I simply smile.

'You on your own?' she asks. 'You saucy mare!'

It takes a moment to realise she assumes I am here in search of a partner.

'I'm here because I want to see the world. My husband died, and I'm not going to sit at home for the rest of my life.' Why am I trying to justify myself?

'You should try the internet,' she insists. 'My friend, she's fifty-five; she found this man on the internet. She meets men on the internet all the time.'

I have no idea how to shut her up. She comes from a world where every single woman must be looking for a man, while I've spent the years since John died proving to my daughters that it is possible to live happily without one.

And – it's true. I am happy without one. Though it's taken a few years to be able to say that. I'm not saying I've lived as a nun, or that I wouldn't appreciate the occasional 'visitor'. But a man who lived in the house with his socks and his snoring and how-about-a-nightcap-darling? No, thank you, I definitely don't want one of those. (Methinks the lady does protest? Not at all – I'm not saying a beautiful Maori doesn't disturb a few sleeping hormones, simply that I don't want to wake up with one every day.)

'I am happy as I am.'

What's the point; she can't believe me.

'You try the internet, you never know what you might find.'

I have to sit next to her for another half an hour; we are, to my relief, diverted by passing a fish market, the smell penetrating even the windows of the bus. But if a British tourist assumes I'm here to look for a partner, maybe local people make the same assumption?

However, in spite of Lolita, in spite of the stupid woman on the bus, Goa does what I need it to do: it gives me respite from thinking. I droop around on beaches, stroll to the markets in Panjim and Anjuna, join a tour around the solid cathedrals of Old Goa. More importantly, I have time to rest.

Resting. Not exciting. I know it makes me sound like a grandmother, needing to put her feet up. But it is necessary. I am overloaded with India. I have landed in Costa del Goa, but the trappings of tourism nurture me safely for a week or two while my body and mind recuperate from the ravages of Rajasthan.

26.

Sonjit meets me at the airport in Cochin, in northern Kerala. He raises his eyes at my tinsel, down to four strands after another flight. I cannot begin to explain. He whisks me, efficiently, to *God's Own Country Home* – run by my travel agent in Mumbai, and situated on the outskirts of Ernakulum. It is newly opened; I am the first guest. The sitting room smells empty; builders tap away in an extension. I wonder how many more hotels I will land in that are not quite finished.

'This is not a hotel,' Sonjit corrects me, 'it is a homestead. I am the manager. This is your home here.' He whistles and the cook, a round-faced, round-bellied man, bustles around me with coconut milk and then coffee. I have to ask his name twice: Chandresh; there seems some surprise that I notice him, but he will frame my week here. He brings me a menu; what would I like for lunch.

'Samosas?' Chandresh looks first at the sky, then at his bare feet, and sighs.

'They take a long time, madam.'

'But it's only half past eleven.'

'They take a ... very ... long time.' He stretches the words out, as if to illustrate how long it might take to prepare samosas.

We agree on pakoras.

'And for supper, madam?'

'I hear the fish curries are good in Kerala.'

'Maybe no fish, madam. The market ...' This time he looks directly at me, as if daring me to insist on fish curry. I struggle to keep a straight face.

'What do you suggest?' And so our dance is orchestrated; I learn the wisdom of suggesting he find what is good in the market, and he cooks what he likes. My reward – the best food of my trip. His curries are better than any I've tasted in the local restaurant; and certainly better than anything I can cook.

If I let them, my daughters would seize this opportunity to list kitchen disasters. My cooking is almost as feeble as my gardening.

Just once, Chandresh honours me with an invitation into the sanctum of his kitchen – not to help, but to inhale as onions and chillies simmer in coconut oil, the sudden pungency of ginger and cardamom and clove. I stand and breathe. For a week I eat like a queen.

I meander towards the city after lunch; it is Saturday; the streets are hot, clammy, and the sewers in full pong. I find an internet café and connect with daughters; sisters are absorbed with preparations for the new baby; plans have changed and he will now be born in the UK. I nurse grand-maternal grief. It is impossible to tolerate, for long, the internal dialogue between my longing to join them, today, this very minute, and the compulsions (for that, I can see, is what it is now) to carry on travelling. I want to knit little cardigans; talk pushchairs and baby baths; discuss the grim details of deliveries. And I want to go south, into the mountains of Kerala, to the backwaters, and on to the bustle of Bangalore. For ten minutes I wonder which wrong thing I should do. With no answer I wander back; it is time for a shower.

I struggle: does the handle turn this way or that for the promised hot water? I climb back into clothes to look for Chandresh.

'Do you know if there is any hot water? I'm probably doing something wrong but I can't make the shower work.'

He abandons his cooking and scurries to my room.

'I didn't mean this minute; I mean, if you are busy ...' He is behaving like a servant but I have no idea how to be a memsahib. Surely compromise must be possible?

'Madam, there must be hot water.' Straight to my bathroom, he stands under the showerhead, fully-clothed, and turns the handle.

'I think it is this way.' He points to the left. 'But maybe, no, it is this way.' Water drips from his collar, from the tip of his nose. I have to turn away so he can't see me stifle a giggle.

'It could have waited.' But my words wash down the drain. I thank him; he sloshes back to the kitchen, and I finally work the shower out for myself.

As I bathe I hear new arrivals; at least I am clean when I meet them. Elica reaches out a hand to greet me.

'Dr Joan, you remember me?'

I trawl through memories of the past few weeks; no, in spite of her 'Dr' clue, her graceful orange sari and manicured nails have left no impression.

'Mumbai?' she tries to help me. 'In the travel agent's? It was me, on the fax machine, organising your journeys. I own the company, and this is my house, my guest house; Dr Joan, you are comfortable here?'

'Very…'

'You like a drink?'

'Do you have a beer?' Elica turns to Chandresh, but he is already scampering towards the kitchen. Seconds later a cold beer is pressed into my hands, but she is scowling.

'There is no napkin; you must serve the beer wrapped in a napkin.' She seizes the beer, hassles Chandresh back into the house; eventually my beer is returned with a soggy napkin clinging to the condensation around the glass. I try to catch his eye; I want to tell him that napkins do not matter, but he hovers, head down, waiting for thanks before he scuttles away.

The only highlight of the evening is supper, which I eat alone: I never work out why Elica insists I eat separately from them. Chandresh presents me (miraculously) with a fish curry; he blossoms when I assure him, truthfully, that it is the best meal I have had in India; he asks me to 'tell her' – which, of course, I do.

I can never resolve the status question. I expect to do things for myself, but, when I drop my napkin on the floor and reach down for it Chandresh races to my side, his face full of hurt. Is he not good enough to pick up my napkin for me? I want to know what brought him here; he must have a story; maybe we could exchange stories, like equals, like proper companions.

'I am a poor man,' he tells me. I have glimpsed his mattress on the floor in the cupboard off the kitchen; he has no space for clothes or mementos. And I have read newspaper advertisements and seen that many of those working in hotels and restaurants are given their food and a place to stay, depending on tips for an income. My comfortable terraced house, back in Wiltshire, would be a palace to him.

'Where did you learn to cook?' I ask, which is what I really want to know. He shrugs; I cannot tell if his misunderstanding is deliberate.

'I do it,' he holds one hand out and circles it with the other, 'for my children, for their education; even what I get here.' He shrugs: 'But the tips ... I am a good man.'

'I know you are', I tell him. I swallow anger – with him, for effectively asking me for money, and – more – at the system which puts him in the position of needing to. It feels like a cruel form of begging.

'I have four children,' he goes on; 'my daughter is very clever; she is fifteen and wants to be a doctor. You will meet her, give her advice. Tomorrow there is a festival; you like to meet my family? You come to the festival; you will meet my daughter and give her advice.'

I am not at all sure what I have agreed to, and Sonjit is sufficiently concerned to insist on coming with us. An oversized car collects us at around six in the evening. We drive out into suburban mayhem – there is new building everywhere, more people, more rubbish, more street stinks. Past the spanking new teaching hospital, with a line of autos and rickety stalls outside, a new IT centre, cows, wandering goats. We stop to collect Chandresh's family: a tiny, disappearing wife and four children; they all squash in the back – I must have the front seat to myself. I am even too important to have a child on my knee, in spite of the discomfort behind me.

We meander towards the festival – which resembles an English fairground. There is a bombardment of colours – plastic flowers, plastic pots, balloons, children's windmills, jewellery; of smells – candy floss, spices, fumes from generators; of noise – motors, hurdy-gurdies, a wall of death with its thunderous motor bikes. There are fairground rides – a pirate ship swinging perilously with no safety straps, rickety aeroplanes for children rising about six foot off the ground, a wooden dragon chuntering round a track. Somehow birds can be heard twittering above the energy and mayhem. The joy of Chandresh and his family is infectious; the younger children shriek on their rides while we tuck into pots of the sweetest popcorn.

Not so different from Marlborough's Mop Fairs, which take over the High Street every October? When the children were small we went every year; we won a goldfish once that lived for three years. They shrieked on the rides, pestered us for candyfloss. I couldn't watch them turned upside-down without my own stomach doing the same. I don't remember if we could hear the birds sing.

Chandresh's daughter is, indeed, delightful. She wanders beside me, reminds me of her medical ambitions; do I have advice for her? I know, at root, what she needs most is money. I am on my own in India; therefore I must be rich. I decide, deliberately, to misread the money question; I shall respond as an older woman, dispensing advice to the young and ambitious. It is not a role that sits comfortably; I am much happier encouraging the young to be frivolous, enjoy the moment, take a gap year. But that, I can see, is inappropriate here. I try to organise a serious expression, make a point of listening intently to her dreams.

'I don't know enough about the system in India to help you,' I say. It is true, but feeble. Try again. 'If it is what you want to do, then you should never give up – India needs good doctors.'

'But you must have advice for me?' Oh dear, her father has prompted her persistence.

'I wish I could help you. But I can see it means a lot to you – so you must take each step at a time; it will take a long time but you must not be disheartened; one day you will get there.' Disappointment creeps across her face; she had hoped for much more than encouragement. I shrink in my inadequacy. All the more so when I know that my 'advice' is meaningless for a family with so little money. It is unlikely she will ever be a doctor, in spite of her intelligence and her dreams. But I cannot rescue her, any more than I could rescue Lolita.

27.

My days in Cochin develop a rhythm. I begin on the balcony, in the sweetest air of the day, with the newspapers. I am greedy for news, as if it might help me make more sense of the general mayhem in the streets. Chandresh plies me with cups of tea.

I should, I know, explore in the cool morning hours. But it is often close to ten thirty before I even make it as far as the bus stop. I am growing to enjoy the buses; although still stared at (I meet no other white women on the buses, and cringe when frail old ladies insist on standing up so I can sit) I am beginning to feel a satisfaction in finding my way around.

But it is hot. Stickily hot. I breathe and the inside of my nose is singed. The air tastes of scorched metal. Floaty clothes cling to me; I have forgotten the embarrassment of damp patches beneath by arms or down my back – there is no point when everything trickles. My feet slide in my sandals. Rings threaten to slip from my fingers. By the end of the day my eyes ache from accommodating the glare of the streets and the sudden gloom of bazaars. And the dust. Everywhere there is dust. In my diary I write, 'I cannot believe I am still talking about the dust.' I can stop talking about it, but carry on coughing.

Nevertheless, I am a different woman from the shrimp of Gorakphur; I don't need to hide any more. I can wander through the turmoil of these streets with confidence and curiosity intact; I can fend off persistent *tuk tuk* drivers and joke with traders demanding I buy their watches or cigarette lighters. The prize: a second-hand bookstall, smelling of mould and old paper, with a pirate copy of Kiran Desai's *The Inheritance of Loss*.

I spend four days exploring the quieter streets of Fort Kochi, with just one serious sight-seeing day. I head south from the ferry towards the Mattancherry Palace. The route takes me through the merchants' quarter where there are dark halls piled high with sacks – a few have labels: there is every different type of rice. I am stung by the sudden pungency of spices, of aniseed, of root ginger, the surprise of heaped herbs. There are piles of bitter teas. I pass a shop selling fragrant oils, but it cannot compete. Goats are shooed away from sacks of potatoes and vegetables.

It is drippingly hot when I reach the Palace. The midday sun glares from cream walls. Inside it is cool, reparative. I am appropriately entranced by carved wooden ceilings, a gallery full of portraits of Cochin's rajahs and busy murals depicting scenes from Hindu stories. But some rooms are being renovated, including one full of pictures of Krishna pleasuring eight maidens at the same time – which is a shame, as it's the closest I'm likely to come to any maidenhead action for a while.

From the Palace to the synagogue, built five hundred years ago and one of the oldest in Asia. Compared with Hindu temples it is simple, almost stark; it is mercifully restful. The floor is laid with Delft tiles, each one different; I cool my feet by studying them for half an hour.

Outside I am greeted by a row of small children, in blue checked shirts, lined up, waiting to go in. They must be about seven years old, eight maybe, chattering in excitement. Two boys tumble against each other; one is holding something (I cannot see what) in a clenched fist and the other tries to seize it. A clutch of little girls bow dark heads together and giggle.

The teacher quells their exuberance with a stern look, and they return to their regimental line. And then they see me. A row of little hands stretch out and they begin a chorus of, 'what is your name? How old are you?' I look across to the teacher and she nods her approval. I make my way down the line, shaking every small hand, catching every pair of brown eyes, trying to remember every name. I wait while a shy boy hides behind his friend for a moment, but then decides he is brave enough to risk experimenting with the texture of my sticky white skin. The smallest girl runs from one end of the line to the other, and manages a second greeting. I pretend that she is shaking my arm off, and the whole class is laughing. I am, eventually, seen off by a line of waving children. The joy of playing! Several hours later and I am still smiling to myself.

The front page of the newspaper the next morning grieves over the death of sixteen children in a lake near the city. They were on a school outing, and, at six in the evening – when it is dark – they had climbed into unlicensed boats for a trip across the lake. There were no life jackets. They were all gathered on an upper deck; one child noticed a leak and tugged on the sleeve of a teacher. She ruffled his hair, told him not to worry, and they set off across the inky water.

I don't know what time the boat went down. Nor did I hear the cries of children as their toes, their knees, their shoulders, their noses disappeared beneath the water. Nor did I watch from another boat, bile in my mouth and screams on my lips, as the floating lights dipped into the lake. I don't know if teachers or boatmen leapt into the night in an effort to hold stretching fingers or resuscitate gasping lips. I don't know who made the phone call asking for help. I do know that it took two hours for the navy to arrive with rescue equipment; local services assessed the situation first, then contacted the navy who had to organise their paraphernalia before setting off.

And there, in the paper, is a picture: a row of sixteen dead children, all wearing blue checked shirts, some still with weed dripping from cuffs and buttons. Beside them the teacher who had nodded her permission for me to play with them.

I am suddenly, incongruously, cold. I don't know how to grieve. Not here. Sitting on an elegant balcony with a newspaper on my knee. There is no one here to agree that this is truly terrible; to struggle for words to describe the horror that children should die so cruelly. No one to join in my anger – at what? At a system that allows children to die needlessly? Or simply that they died at all. I want to shout about it, to wail, have a tender arm around my shoulders while I sob. Instead I just sit. Maybe such feelings can only find real expression when they are given a voice, and listened to. For once my diary is not strong enough. I can only stare at the picture in the paper, and dare to imagine how their parents are feeling this morning. I wish I could tell them that, in the afternoon at least, their children were playing.

There are countless letters; one insists that standards must improve as tourists might gather a poor impression of India from incidents such as these.

28.

It is time to move on. Kuljeet arrives to drive me around the sights of Kerala. He is a barrel-chested man, his dark skin pock-marked; he wears a sparkling white shirt and pressed trousers. (How does he keep so clean? My clothes have assumed a uniform colour of dust.)

His hand rests on the bonnet of a Scorpio Turbo. This, I learn, is to be my chariot for the next few weeks. It is twice as big as the Renault I sold before coming away. I turn to Sonjit, but he replies before I can phrase my question.

'You will be pleased with a big car in the mountains; some of the roads are not good. You will be comfortable in this.' I suspect an appeasement of the status god. Later I learn that Kuljeet saves money by sleeping in the car and am relieved he has some comfort at night.

We are both determined to enjoy this journey. He seizes my hand, and with it comes a deep, back-of-the-throat laugh. We are off.

'What are you called?' He used 'madam' before we left; now he calls me 'Jo'.

'My driving? It is good?' I assure him that his driving is fine.

'Not too fast? Not too slow?'

(What instructions has he been given? Has someone pulled the 'Professor' rank again, and he thinks I'm some dignitary?)

'You drive in your country?' he asks.

'Yes, I drive, but I do not have a car now; I sold that before I left.'

'You drive fast?'

'I used to drive fast, when I was younger.' He bursts into his generous laugh. I elect not to tell him about my first car, an ancient Morris Minor, which I would allow – just once a year – to show its paces on the motorway. It never made it over eighty. He asks how old I am, what work I do, and do I have family. Questions that would seem intrusive at home, but don't worry me here. I am curious about him, and it is only fair that I contribute my stories as well. I talk about my daughters; he asks if they are married and I lie.

'Do you arrange marriages in your country?'

'No, we let young people work it out for themselves.'

'It never lasts,' he scowls. 'They will get divorced in two years. Here we arrange marriage. People stay together.' I take his point; it is not a conversation I want to explore too deeply. My own divorce was so long ago it feels like someone else's story; my ex-husband and I can talk about mistakes now, wish each other well. We make good friends. But I have no idea how to explain that to Kuljeet.

We are driving away from the dust of Cochin and pass by a field of cashew nut trees, with their tiny red and yellow fruit that smell of apple. He rises to my interest, stopping at every field opportunity: bananas, coconut palms, pepper trees – peppercorns hot enough to make me sneeze and growing in long strings, rubber trees – the sap (he calls it milk) dripping into coconut shells, to be collected later and made into small sheets that are hung like washing on a line, mango trees, fields of spiky pineapples. This is the garden of India.

'You grow bananas in your country?'

'No, it is too cold for bananas.' He is baffled.

'Too cold? How is it too cold?'

'It is too cold for many things. We grow potatoes and wheat and many vegetables, but we cannot grow bananas.' He tuts to himself; I am not sure he believes me. He pulls over again; I assume there is another field to inspect and open the door.

'No; I am making the urine,' he tells me. I keep my eyes to the front.

His astonishment continues when he returns. 'You have wild animals in England?'

'Yes, we have many animals. We have badgers and foxes, and deer.'

'Elephants?'

'No, there are no elephants.'

'No elephants!?'

'No elephants, nor tigers, nor monkeys.'

He struggles. 'How many seasons do you have?' I try to explain four seasons, falter over thoughts of lambs and daffodils in springtime, lurching with an unexpected longing for Wiltshire and her Downs.

Kuljeet takes no notice of my verbal stumbling. 'When is

your monsoon?'

'We don't have a monsoon.' Now he is sure I am fibbing. A country with no elephants and no monsoon is more than his mind can cope with. He breaks into his great laugh.

'You are ready for lunch? You like a big hotel, or a small one? The big hotel is very expensive.'

'And the small hotel?'

'I am a poor man.' We agree on the small hotel. He finds a dark café. Taxi and *tuk tuk* drivers sit at wobbly tables. There is a smell of curry and grime and men. I am the only woman and they stare at me. But I am used to it; it feels ordinary now. We find a spare table; Kuljeet walks to a sink at the back of the room to wash his hands, and I copy him. Plates are plonked on the table and a man walks between us with a hefty bowl of rice, another with dahl and vegetables, filling plates as he passes. Kuljeet rolls it all together and eats easily with his fingers. I am allowed a spoon – in my three months in India I never manage finger-eating without my hands, mouth and lap smothered in embarrassment.

I pay the bill and we are on our way again.

'Do you like drink?' he asks. 'Beer? Whisky? Rum?'

'I like a beer in the evenings; do you know if I can get a beer in my hotel?'

'It is expensive in the hotel, isn't it; in the government shop it cost sixty, seventy rupees; in the hotel two times, three times that. You ask me; I will buy you beer. Then you hide it when you go in, drink in your room. You buy in the hotel and they will cheat you.' We agree the beer-buying plan.

'Right, and if I buy one for me, you will not tell them?' he asks.

'I don't understand. What is the problem with you having a drink?'

'You tell them, in Cochin, I will lose my job.' I wonder if we are struggling with language here, but his face is clouded and he clearly needs reassurance.

'Surely what you do when we have finished driving is nothing to do with me. You keep me safe in the daytime; at night you do as you wish.'

'You will not tell them in Cochin?' His voice is thick with anxiety.

'If you are drunk in the morning I will tell them. But what you do in your own time is up to you – I will not tell.'

'My job, I must be ready to drive you all the time.' I begin to understand. He is paid to be available at any moment, must be on duty day and night.

'I do not need you all the time. When we are not driving, you can do as you please.' He is sufficiently reassured to buy plenty of beer.

We fall into comfortable ways. His questions continue. I understand curiosity and answer him readily. And he takes predictable opportunities to exploit our relationship.

Maybe exploit is too pejorative a word; it grows from a western attitude to baksheesh. He negotiates elephant rides, boat trips, a trek up a mountain in a jeep, Kathakali dancing (traditional Keralan theatre) and I know he lines his own pocket as we go. Most of the time I am able to shrug, knowing this is how the world goes round in India. But we fall out over my massage.

'Agent has booked massage in the hotel? In Thekkady?' He searches my papers. Yes, a massage has been agreed.

'You be careful. You ask questions. Many hotels, they use old oil. You need new oil, not oil has been on many bodies. It is your body. You must ask for new oil.'

We trundle on, but he cannot leave the massage question.

'And you ask, are they learning? It is your body. You don't want someone who is learning. I find you massage, someone who massage for many years. Fresh oil.'

I begin to see where this is going. I promise to ask all the right questions.

'It is your choice. You ask them. New oil, not old oil. And

no learners. And ask to see a doctor. They must see you are healthy. Not all hotels have doctor. It is your body.'

'It is my choice,' I remind him.

We are racing towards Thekkady, Kuljeet's driving transformed from his normal serene style into Indian furore. He parks and rushes me into a massage parlour.

'Just look,' he says, and turns away.

The proprietor has already waved brochures in front of me, prices (one thousand rupees for an Ayurvedic massage) in tiny letters on the back.

'I show you rooms, no problem,' he insists. I agree to look at a room; it contains a blue couch and smells of plastic. It does not alarm me, but I am adamant I have no time now, and walk out – looking for Kuljeet.

A man in the doorway tells me he is moving the car and will be back.

And so I stand, in the doorway of a massage parlour, with no idea where I am, where Kuljeet is, nor how I might get back to the hotel. If I were younger I might have worried. As it is, I know no one will misread my wrinkles.

Kuljeet, however, is thunderous when he reappears. I have obviously deprived him of a hefty slice of the price.

'Lunch,' I say, smartly. 'We need lunch before the boat trip at two.'

'You like massage here?'

'We have no time.'

'It is your choice. Maybe tomorrow.' He shuffles, then stands squarely.

We prickle over lunch.

I have an Ayurvedic massage at the hotel. Two women smother me in warm oil. They are horrified when I ask if anyone ever does this for them. They, it seems, are from a caste that gives massage, and cannot conceive of a right to receive one.

Kuljeet and I pack up to leave Thekkady.

'The massage, it was fine?' He is almost spitting at me.

'Yes, it was fine.'

'No learners? No body pain?'

'No, no learners. And no body pain.'

'Last night, beer then dinner?'

'No, dinner, then beer. I went back to my room to watch England win at cricket.' At last, he guffaws. We both understand the importance of cricket.

29.

The massage is soon forgotten. And there are no complaints when I ask him to help me find a project where my brother worked over thirty years ago. I know its name – Mitraniketan; it is a community and school; somewhere near the village of Vellanad, itself not far from Thiruvananthapuram (known as Trivandrum), a major city in southern Kerala. Kuljeet is unstinting in his effort to help me find it.

We drive through the mayhem of Trivandrum and out into the wooded hills beyond. He stops to ask; he asks again. We go the wrong way through this village, then the right way through that, and finally we are directed up a narrow road to find a mishmash of buildings sheltered under towering trees. The ground is littered with leaf debris; the air – we are higher here – smells of pine.

I have my spiel ready – my brother was here many years ago; was very happy; and so I want to call by. I stumble into the nearest open doorway to find myself in the library, with just five people reading books and newspapers; my opening lines falter in the quiet. It is a dark room, cool, with books overflowing shelves and piled on the floor; there is a smell of damp paper. A young woman offers to take me to the director's wife, Sadu – who, to my astonishment is the same director's wife my brother knew. It takes her just a minute to realise who I am talking about and then her welcome is unreserved.

'How long can you stay?'

'Not long; my driver will take me back to Kovalam tonight.'

'You should have brought your luggage; stayed here.'

'I didn't know what to expect.' She is eager to show me.

After weeks negotiating the worst of India's streets, I am captivated by the efforts at Mitraniketan. It began as a non-profit-making school for pupils who were disadvantaged in some way – through poverty or caste or disability – and all from rural areas. The emphasis on education for the excluded continues. There is a kindergarten for under-fives, followed by places for up to three hundred children to receive formal education. We pass a group of girls returning from an exam-room; there are a few giggled 'hellos' but not one request for a school pen. Young people who continue to struggle at the end of formal education are offered a place in the People's College, with its vocational courses. The aim is to provide all students with skills that they can use in their villages – agriculture, food processing, carpentry. I am shown a clattering sewing room, full of young women bent over machines like the one my mother used (it is in my roof-space, even now), tables littered with Indian fabrics in bright reds and blues and gold. Ancient typewriters clank in another hut. Three students, covered in grease and smelling of machines, have stripped down a motorbike. There is a pottery, a woodshed, a smithy where students learn to make tools.

It covers a vast campus, spread across a brown hillside cooled by a breeze easing between coconut palms, criss-crossed by tracks and roadways (roadways my brother built), and includes accommodation for staff and visitors. There are plants everywhere and I can identify none of them. It breathes with purpose, and with fun. Staff grin as they pass me by; children chatter, play tag along pathways; women flush as I admire sewing or a page of type. It still makes no profit. It is a glorious antidote to the touts and beggars of the cities.

I wish I could stay longer – and Sadu wants to keep me. But I am anxious about Kuljeet; he has a long way to drive today.

Sadu urges me to linger to meet Vishwan, who founded this project. He is frail now but still tall with penetrating eyes, dressed in a white shirt and *dhoti*. He is magnetic; in spite of his frailty I can see the passion that gathered the small band that turned his vision into the magic of Mitraniketan. He, too, remembers my brother, who obviously made an impression on these gentle people. Vishwan is almost accusatory as he asks why I am rushing off. And I feel guilt at leaving.

I reflect in the air-conditioned cool of my hotel room. Could I return there, work for a few weeks before my flight from Chennai? I flirt with the idea of changing arrangements. A quick phone call to Mumbai, a reorganised train ticket (not straightforward, but then nothing is in India); it would be easy to step into my brother's shoes and spend a few weeks here. Well, maybe my road-building days are behind me, but I can type, use a sewing machine, play with children.

But I have seen the dormitories where the volunteers sleep, the meagre beds, the cold showers. There are no other volunteers there at the moment. Am I ready for that level of discomfort? In spite of the challenges of India I have always been able to keep clean, and to retreat to a room of my own when the sensory mayhem around me gets too much. Thirty years ago – I'd have gone, without a second thought. Chucked my rucksack on a bunk bed, hitched up my skirts, prepared to spend weeks covered in dust. I'd have lugged stones to help build the road; taught the children; planted rice; drunk tea with the women.

Now? Now I am not that brave. With only Sadu and Vishwan who speak English I'd be in linguistic limbo; I'm not sure I can cope with that for long. On top of that I know that I relish the unfamiliar provided there is enough comfort to fall back on. My adolescent curiosity does not translate into a middle-aged capacity to cope with too much deprivation. I still need to keep one foot in my European ways.

I am not proud of these feelings. There is a whiff of

condescension about them. I do not like myself for it, but that is how it is.

30.

We drive on to Kumerakom, a village on the edge of Lake Vembanad in the backwaters of Kerala: a flatland criss-crossed with waterways and canals, opening into the still waters of the lake. It is steamily hot. Traditional rice-ferries have been transformed into houseboats for tourists; we watch as one chugs by with a couple sipping wine beneath their rush shelter in the bows while a puffing man pumps water that has leaked into the hold at the stern. (I read in the paper that there has been an inspection: of the seventy houseboats on the backwaters forty-six have failed. None are removed from service. No one is surprised.)

We have agreed that Kuljeet should have a day off. It is a new idea for him, but he does not argue. I am relieved to be out of the car for a day – and am sure he is equally pleased to have a day away from me. I meander into the village. Boys are leaping into the canal; there is the pretence of soap. Women crouch by steps with bowls full of pots and pans to wash. The water is brown, thick with reeds and laced with traces of diesel. It smells, mostly, of reeds, with occasional brackish crannies.

I cross a bridge to investigate a church. A weathered man is watering some forlorn plants and I pause to admire his efforts; he is more successful in this dust than I am in the fertile soil of Wiltshire. Geraniums splash red across the forecourt, surviving somehow in the cracked earth. He grins and asks where I am from. I assume we are about to embark on the now-familiar conversation about my origins and family when he beckons me beyond his garden.

In front of me is a large village hall, with rows of empty seats and one narrow platform where about twenty-five little girls, in red checked dresses, are practising their dancing, apparently for some sort of display. The gardener urges me into a chair and then slides away. It is pointless trying to hide: I feel like the last swimmer stranded on the beach. Besides, the children and their teacher have seen me, and so I pretend to be parents, clapping and stamping my solitary appreciation when the dance comes to an end. My efforts dissipate in the cavern of the hall, but the children seem delighted anyway.

I wave my camera towards the stage – may I take a photo? The teacher hurries a small group of children to pose for me; they rush back to my side in a wave of giggles to look at the result. They lean on my knees, smelling of soap and powder, and pull at my hands to get a look at the camera. It is wonderful to be surrounded by children – they don't care if I'm old or young, pink or blue, if I will play with them. My working days are behind me; now I can revel in the sheer joy of this gaggle of little girls. But I have gatecrashed a lesson and there is now a risk that girlish excitement (theirs and mine) will disrupt proceedings even more. I find a hundred rupee note to give to the teacher, waving to indicate that it should be spread among all the children, and turn to leave.

Little girls come racing after me, grab my hands, and pull me back into the hall. Their teacher, elegant in her purple sari but with no English, seems equally insistent. She waves me up onto the stage, to stand with the children. They are clustered around me; one pulls at the back of my shirt but shrinks when I swing round to face her. Another cannot restrain herself: she must stroke my arm to see what it feels like. They cannot have enough of my hair. I restrain the urge to play, looking to the teacher for clues as to what might come next.

It seems that I must join their dance. The CD player clicks. Indian rhythms echo in the hall.

I try. I manage the step and stamp and back and stamp. I manage the move that involves a bit of a hop. I can slip to the side and the front and round again. The problem comes when they try to teach me the hand moves. My ring finger cannot stand tall if the second is tucked into my hand. The teacher shows me, shows me again. One little girl tries holding my hand and forcing my fingers to conform, but her efforts are curtailed when we both disintegrate into giggles.

The brave teacher gives up. I am too useless (or disobedient) even to join the lumpy girl at the back. I watch them from a privileged position on the stage and clap as if it were the last night of the Proms when their display is done. They set themselves as if to dance again, but this time I am determined to leave. I am unsure if I am still welcome – the teacher has a lesson to complete and I cannot read her signals. I will never know if I should have stayed. Two months in India is not long enough to understand the subtlety of her cues.

I can hear the music, and girlish giggles, far down the canal bank. A kingfisher streaks across the water, filling the air with iridescence. For days I try the finger-thing, but never master it. I asked no questions, and discovered no answers beyond the sheer delight of dancing with children.

PART FIVE

DEFEATED BY INDIA

31.

Kuljeet has gone. Again I need solitary time to reorient myself. My hotel backs onto a beach south of Kovalam. I drift out of the back gate, hoping to paddle for a while before supper. There is a scrubby patch of grass between the hotel and silver sand of the beach. Boys in orange shirts are playing football.

Four boys, aged about ten to twelve years old, materialise beside me. Where am I from? Where is my husband? Where am I staying? These are familiar questions and open easy banter. Besides, they are children. I understand children. They ask if I support Manchester United and for the first time in India I find someone who knows nothing about cricket.

'And where do you live?' I asked. They wave along the beach.

'Adimalathura. It is not far.'

We are strolling towards a small church, perched about fifty feet above the sea on rocks at the end of the beach. The sun is beginning to stain the sky with pink; there is just enough breeze to loosen my hair and rustle the great leaves of the coconut palms. The sea is quiet, unthreatening. There is nowhere else I would rather be. The boys reach out their hands to guide me as we clamber up uneven steps.

'We look after you. You are our grandmother. Whenever you come to the beach we will help you.' My wrinkles, it seems, are badges of honour. I grin, limp a little, reach out for support as if I were eighty, not a mere fifty-seven. We mime our mutual delight.

The light is sinking, and we are making our way back when a second group of boys rounds the headland.

My new friends speed up a little. 'They are bad boys. They do not go to school. They are very bad – they will ask you for school pens.' Their previous bravado amuses me; one hint of a threat and they seem to want to hide under my wings.

And then comes a call from behind us: 'I will kill you (he means me). I must kill you because you are with bad boys.' He is wielding a piece of driftwood, but his logic entertains me and I don't feel intimidated. I worked with boys like this, who had had terrible things happen to them and needed to assault the world. I respond in the only way I know how.

'You are telling me that they are the bad boys, and so you must kill me?' I reply, with no more drama in my voice than if he had suggested I join him for a cup of tea and is sorry that I have a better idea. He nods. Then turns away. Only then do I wonder what I would have done if he had smacked me round the head with his driftwood. My new friends are still behind me, but cluster as the bully slinks away. As the situation settles they tell me that the wood-waving lad had been drinking, I must take no notice of him.

'We would defend you,' they insist, 'if he had hit you.' I do not believe them; yet I dare not entertain an image of myself bloodied on an Indian beach. They assure me that they are not bad boys. I have no idea who might be a bad boy and who good; and maybe it doesn't matter. We have played, talked football; they have treated me like the Queen Mother.

We have reached the back gate of the hotel and I turn to leave them.

'Before you go, you will see us again?'

'Maybe I will see you again.'

'You buy us books for school? We can show you the shop. It is not far from here. We will take you there.' There is a moment's disappointment at their ulterior motive, and then I recall the fun we have had. I make no promises and return to my room to think how I might help them.

They pounce on me next time I leave.

'You will buy us books for school?'

'No, but I'd like to visit your school and buy something for all the children.'

'No, you cannot do that. It is too far. You cannot walk there.'

'I like walking. If it is not too far for you, then it is not too far for me.'

'But if you give money to the teachers they steal it. They never spend money on the children. You must give it to us. Or you can meet our father, and give it to him.'

'I would really like to visit your school, to talk to the teachers myself.'

'No!' they cry in unison. They are determined to keep me well away from their school. I am caught – between wanting to do something for them (the cost of a few books and pens is minimal here), but this is beginning to smell like a scam. I cannot tell where truth lies. I retreat, trying to think of another plan.

The shop is easy to find. It is at the front of the hotel. There are crumpled packs of pens and books which seem to be bought by tourists and given to the boys, who then sell them back to the shop. A lucrative business, a wily exploitation of the guilt of tourists faced with the impossible poverty of India?

I can see these boys from my balcony. There is a group of about twenty of them, working in groups of four or five. They sidle up to every tourist as they leave the back gate, chat with the enthusiasm that has entranced me, and then corner them at the back gate with the, 'will you give us ...' question. I can see they are given pens and books; one man gives them a football. There is no evidence that they attend school at all.

They trouble me. Their activities are harmless now. But I worry about their leering at the young women, clad in the scantiest of bikinis, who strut along the beach in search of a tan. These boys are used to manipulating tourists to get what they want. Most visitors seem oblivious to the game that is played. What will happen when adolescent hormones drive them in more dangerous directions? I don't suppose I'd find them so playful then.

32.

I wake early one morning. It is already warm, but the air is fresh, crisp, inviting. I seize my camera and make for the beach, looking for photographs in the silver dawn light. I pad across the patch of grass, kept short by barefoot football-players and the occasional cow, towards the sea. There are no boys here this early in the morning.

I had thought I would have the beach to myself. How foolish. From the cliff top I have seen fishing boats scattered like flotsam on the sand; when did I think they went to sea? At the water's edge I find teams of sweating men heaving huge nets, each about two miles long. Boats have dragged the centre of the nets out into the bay, and now lines of men seize each end and slowly haul them into semicircles and so back towards the shore. Here are entire villages of men: from the lithe and muscular to withered and phlegmy. Each man heaves his section of rope backwards from the sea to an anchorman, who arranges the rope into coils like giant worm casts. The pulling men run back to the front, pick up the next section of rope, and drag it backwards again. And as they haul they chant: 'waa da wabberly waa ba lay', or something like that!

I take photographs from what I hope is a respectful distance. But, without warning, they pick up the rope and coil, and rush about twenty feet up the beach. A young man in red shorts waves to me to follow them. There is more waving – and suddenly I gather their meaning: I can join in! I know that hauling ropes is not women's work in India, and certainly not for wrinklies, but I need no second invitation. Two men slip sideways to make room for me. One particularly shrivelled man wearing dark green shorts and with more wisps of grey hair on his chest than his head prompts me when it is time to leave my rope with the coil man and run back to the front of the line. He always ensures there is a space for me.

At first I think I can keep my skirt dry. Quite how I thought I could cling to such niceties I've no idea. Maybe the memory of being told off by my mother when, at the age of five, I played in a local pond with all my clothes on, has left a lasting taste. But the absurdity of such optimism is too apparent and after just two pulls I wade into the sea with the others. Wet skirts – pah! Even my mother would get a wet skirt here. The rope is rough; the sand gritty between my toes; sweat drips from the end of my nose. The gulls are shrieking. We pull and move up, pull and move up. My skirt grips my knees; my shirt clings to my back. Euphoria sweeps across my mind. This is hard work, and I feel privileged to have been invited to share it.

Eventually the thick rope gives way to a cluster of thinner strings and suddenly the air is full of leaping fish, diving in and out of the sea in the hope of escape, a flapping silver dance that lasts less than a minute. There seems to be nothing but fish and sweat and sea.

I am eventually waved to one side, and pointed to where the Indian women are waiting with their steel bowls glittering in the morning sunlight. For the first time I feel awkward. The men have sanctioned my pleasure but these women, with their ragged red saris and bare feet, are unimpressed.

It gets worse. I stand aside while the men finally haul the nets onto the beach and tip buckets of fish into waiting tubs. Most of the fish are less than thirty centimetres long and will make a puny meal; few are as big as a well-fed mackerel – these are put to one side, presumably for sale. These tubs are then carried up the beach and emptied into heaps beside the women. Selling is women's work.

When I left my room this morning I carried only my camera. I have no money. I have been welcomed into the bric-a-brac of village life. One woman, a baby at her hip, holds out a fish, two fishes, her eyes imploring me to buy them. The hotel is now twenty minutes away and already they are packing up to return to their huts among the coconut palms. I have nothing to give them.

I slink away. Along the beach I pass another pale tourist, a solid woman in beige skirt and white shirt, waving her arms at the fishermen as if trying to conduct an orchestra.

'No,' she cries, 'it is easier if you do it this way.'

My only consolation is that I did as I was told.

I retreat into Kovalam, and then to Trivandrum to buy a train ticket. It is a rigmarole but not a problem. To think I once needed Tika's help to cross the road!

But I have not learned to read people here. I am still stared at, occasionally followed. This does not feel threatening any more, rather an expression of curiosity. But I have been on the edge of so many scams here, and cannot – in the instant of meeting someone – read whether they are honest. The boys on the beach, in spite of their apparent playfulness, want only to exploit me. The fishermen were generous, though I am sure they had hoped for money – and had a right to it, given the pleasure they gave me. I let them down.

I make another mistake on the bus back to Kovalam. It is, as usual, crammed with people. A man with one leg hops on, unaided, leans against a chair without assistance, and hops off two stops later. I feel as if I am the only person to have noticed. I clutch a slippery pole (it is difficult to keep myself steady when my hands are so sweaty); a woman reaches out her hand to hold my water bottle for me while I rifle my purse for change. I have no hesitation in trusting her, yet cannot – even reflecting afterwards – know how I know that.

Then a man stands up, signalling me to his seat. I am

surprised – it means sitting next to a young man, a rare proximity of genders in India.

He begins with familiar questions (though I cannot take my eyes from his elegant hands). 'Where is your husband?'

Whoppers come more easily to me now.

'He is in the hotel; he is not well today but knows I am coming back soon.'

'And your children?'

'They are in England? (At least that is true.) Do you work here?' I try to slip away from fibbing.

'I do massage. You hear of Ayurvedic massage?' That explains his beautiful hands.

'Yes; I had a massage in the mountains. You work in a resort?'

'Where do you eat?' Why his sudden change of subject? Alarm bells begin to ring. Where is this conversation heading?

'I eat in the hotel.'

'You could eat with me. I have a home near here.' He presses his hands together; his fingers are long and musical. How much further till I get off the bus?

'My husband is waiting for me; we always eat in the hotel.' Would John understand this sudden need to resurrect him? Create a myth around his eating habits?

'You like Indian food? At my house we have good Indian food.'

'We always eat in the hotel. My husband likes to eat there.' He asks where I get off; it is his stop, too. An elephant, chains clanking between her back legs, is plodding up the other side of the road. I turn back from watching it and am surprised that he is still beside me.

I have misjudged him; he holds out his hand for me to shake (oh, those hands), a firm, definitive handshake.

'I am sorry you cannot come to my house. My wife would like to meet you.' He strides up the road and I mourn at his retreating back. I sink at the side of the road, flirt briefly with the idea of racing after him, explaining that my whole story was a fabrication and, yes, I would love to meet his wife. But what sort of plonker would I have looked then?

I have been in India well over two months and still have no idea how to recognise people I can trust. It makes India hard work.

33.

Time to move on again. I fly to Bangalore, the state capital of Karnataka. The journey is uneventful; and four feeble strands of tinsel still survive.

I am not sure why I have come to Bangalore. Probably it is because Vedesh insisted that I should visit. He is proud, I suspect, of the economic hurdles that have been vaulted to bring prosperity here. It is the engine of India's boom, her silicon valley, her call centre. A sparkling new airport is under construction; a metro system is planned. I find international restaurants, theatres, huge cinemas sporting Bollywood posters and crowds of young men shouting in their doorways. Such a contrast to the slums of Mumbai. But still light years away from Wiltshire.

Every morning, as I write in my diary, I ask myself the same question.

I know I can do this now – so why am I still here? When spring is spreading her tender fingers across Wiltshire's Downs; when daughters are counting down to the arrival of a new baby. Sometimes I count the weeks until I can go home, as if there were some sort of prize in surviving for a whole year. There is nothing to stop me going home, except, perhaps, a loss of face – which might have worried me twenty years ago, but certainly not now.

Surely, given that I know, now, that I am capable of travelling on my own, that doesn't mean that I have to carry on doing it.

And yet, once breakfast is over and I'm back in the streets I know there is nowhere else I'd rather be. I'm no longer doing this because I can. But also because now, even here in India with all its contradictions, I am excited by every bus journey, every unexpected conversation, every unpredictable street.

It is easy to catch the bus from my hotel to MG Road. (Every town and city in India has an MG – Mahatma Gandhi – Road.) I am standing near the front, close enough to notice that the driver sits with a newspaper on his knee. As the traffic chokes to a standstill for the third time I can see why. A half-built flyover, with no sign of workers but a complete forest of road cones, dictates to the traffic. Pollution is thick enough to cut.

One side of MG Road is taken up by a giant parade ground, lined with sleeping families and barefoot children. A mother, slumped in the shade of a scrawny tree, urges her toddler towards me; he wipes his nose on his arm and stretches out a filthy hand.

Across the road – eight lanes of undisciplined traffic – are shops: inviting, air-conditioned shops. Young men in jeans strut along the pavements. Young women in jeans follow them. Some men, in suits and clutching laptop-cases, thread an urgent path through the crowds. And there are women – fewer, but they are there – in modest western dress.

I scan the faces of the elderly. Well, I say elderly as if they are ancient, when in truth I have no idea how old they are; I don't know the life expectancy in India, but I doubt if many will outlive me. Some of these wizened men and women might just be collecting their pensions at home. But they have seen such huge social changes – many more than I have. I can remember black and white televisions and airmail letters; their memories must struggle to link these thrusting streets of Bangalore with the traditions of rural India that ruled for so long. Suddenly I feel almost young. Old men sit heavily in dark cafés; old women cuddle into their saris and scowl. Prosperity has its price.

At one end of MG Road I find 'Bangalore Central': a five-storey department store smelling of perfume. There is a discreet coffee shop on a mezzanine floor and I find a refuge in the familiar. I could be in Swindon. Though – on closer inspection, maybe not. I find two floors dedicated to clothes for men, and just half a floor for women. The section given over to young people is full of shirts and jeans for lads with a half-hidden corner of blouses and skirts for young women. The newspapers insist gender equality has arrived in Bangalore, but men still hold the purse-strings.

Another day, and I am joined for breakfast by Barry, an American businessman, and Otto, his German colleague. They are struggling to negotiate with an Indian company. At home they would have hidden behind newspapers or chatted together as if I weren't there. In this bleak breakfast room they are looking for comfort from anyone, even from me.

'We've come to sort out a contract,' Barry tells me. 'We had an arrangement with them and it seems some components aren't working properly. Every time we arrange a meeting there is another problem. There are no parts available; they will cost this, no they will cost that. We can't get hold of so-and-so, he is in Mumbai, or New Delhi – anywhere but here. Every time we think we've made progress something else is wrong.'

'I have promised to be home,' Otto contributes. 'Twice I promise to be home, and still I am here. I will never work here again. It is impossible.'

'Maybe,' – suddenly I feel like an old hand at India – 'there is benefit to them in keeping you here. The company makes work and this hotel makes more money. India does things differently.' Barry mutters his disbelief.

'Look how many men are employed here.' I wave my hand at the line standing idly behind the breakfast bar. 'The longer you stay here, the more people can be given work. It doesn't help them if everything is resolved quickly.' This is alien to Barry's American thinking, and he responds by repeating his list of difficulties.

'Maybe, if you threaten to leave, the parts might miraculously appear?' I suggest. They seem unconvinced, though I can see they might think about it later. I used to be irritated by men who pooh-poohed ideas from a woman, only to take them up later as if they were their own. Now, I find it mildly amusing. A driver arrives to collect them and I wish them well.

The next morning I meet Barry and Otto again. They threatened to leave and suddenly have made some progress; soon they can go home.

'But not today, not for three days, they tell us. There is a festival and there will be no flights. So we have to stay until next week.' No flights? None at all? From Bangalore? Do they really believe this?

'Are you sure there are no flights? Remember – you are worth more money to them here than on your way home?' But a manager has assured them, and offered a car for a couple of days (I don't ask what this costs) to take them sightseeing. Otto is grimly resigned.

I bump into them later in MG Road.

By now Otto is raging. 'We were taken to a temple – but saw nothing. At every turn they ask for money, money for guide, money for *bindi*, money for flowers – they want nothing but our money, we can't stop to look at anything unless we pay for it. Even in the temple.'

I hope that a walk in Cubbin Park will comfort him; odd, that I should behave like a mother with a child who is in a bad mood. Through Victorian iron gates, and we stroll between flowerbeds aflame with zinnia and geraniums. It is the weekend and the paths are alive with families; children run from swings to slides to creaking roundabouts; street vendors call attention to their balloons and popcorn and sugar cane juice; a skinny horse offers rides. We ignore the acrid stink of smouldering rubbish; Otto takes photographs with a long lens that seem, to me, intrusive; but he is, at last, in better humour.

Barry takes snaps and buys ice cream. It is the stuff of weekends.

34.

There is nothing to keep me in Bangalore. It is an easy bus ride to Mysore. And, to my surprise, it is the first time I find myself loving an Indian city. It is an enthusiastic, animated metropolis. Art galleries and theatres celebrate Asian culture; universities are proud to boast the only engineering college set aside for women in India. I chat to a woman on a bus: she is clutching a chemistry textbook and will graduate soon; she hopes to be a professor one day. (Maybe she should speak to Vedesh!)

There is too much to see. The main streets are wide, airy, with space to move, even though the air is ripe with city fumes: urine, traffic, ponies. Old colonial buildings, graciously painted in clean cream, jostle with shacks and huts and tumbling stalls. I pass a line of men crouched over old Olivetti typewriters; others are clattering on rickety Singer sewing machines. There are rows of shops selling toilet bowls, then a section devoted to parts for motorbikes. One street is devoted to glorious saris; on another the jewellers flourish behind bars and barricades. On three occasions I am invited to make my way to a café selling, 'you know, like Glastonbury, like incense, like Amsterdam, it is legal here.' I resist. Even though being mistaken for an aging hippy is not unflattering.

I wander towards the Jaganmohan Palace and Art Gallery; I want to see the largest collection of pictures and artefacts in Mysore. I anticipate vast paintings of the Hindu epics, murals, sculptures, ancient instruments such as those that once accompanied the Kathakali. But, as I make it into the palace grounds, I am distracted by the call of music, follow its lure and slip inside a hall as big as an airport lounge. It takes a moment for my eyes to adjust to the half-light. There is a smell of space. Ahead of me the floor slopes gently downwards. Above – a gallery.

Was this once a royal auditorium? Rows of chairs face a stage at the far end of the hall. I pause at the door; there are people sitting, wandering around, drifting in and out; no one collecting money. I slide into a seat, unnoticed. For the first time in India I am invisible; it is a familiar state, and I know how to exploit it. I retrieve my diary from the bottom of my bag and scribble.

I can't work out if this is some sort of dress rehearsal (which would explain why people are walking in and out) or a final performance. A video camera is trained on the stage and its manipulator waves irate arms at a man who stands in front of him to take photographs. There is occasional laughter and applause, but it seems to me disorganised, haphazard.

I am transfixed by the flamboyance on the stage. The scene seems to be set in a dazzling room in a palace, lined with pillars painted in red and gold. There are just three coloured spotlights – red, blue and yellow, which take turns reflecting from a mirror ball to flitter sparkles across the stage. In addition, a display of fairy lights dangling from the ceiling rivals American homes at Christmas. Scene shifters dart across behind the actors.

Time for action. A swarthy man strides on, looks towards the wings and then sidles back the way he came, as if hoping no one has noticed his arrival. He is replaced by a beautiful couple – she is in scarlet and gold, and he's in gold and dripping with brilliant orange garlands; they hold swinging hands and sing.

This couple slide off (they never return and I have no idea what role they take in the action) and the first man takes their place. He is resplendent in red and gold trousers, his bare chest heavy with bling; he has a large black moustache and a sonorous voice – I decide he must be a baddie. (Maybe I watched too many pantomimes as a child.) He sings a song, but gives no clues as to its meaning. Off he goes.

The scene shifters groan and grunt, pushing a couch off to one side and hauling a polystyrene stone, which squeaks its way across the floor, in from the other. Columns totter sideways, replaced by cardboard trees. It is the turn of three maidens. There is more glitter and more singing. Three women hold hands and sigh. Two kiss their friend goodbye; the third is left alone to sit on the rock.

And so it goes on. Wobbly scenery enters left; glitter enters right. An orange bird, one wing flopping alarmingly, jerks down from the ceiling. Somewhere in the audience a man whistles. A stagehand crawls in to pick it up a stray garland.

I clap on cue, and swing my shoulders and tap my feet to the music, absorbed in the colours and the energy and mystery of it all. I watch for almost two hours, love every minute of it, and have no idea at all what is going on. That doesn't matter; not any more.

When I left home I might have raced to the Internet, searched the pages of my *Lonely Planet*, looking for the myth that may underpin this story. Now – I've enjoyed myself. My ignorance is irrelevant. I left home with a list of questions, things I hoped to discover. India has presented me with more questions than answers – except the one that matters most. I know now that I can make huge travelling mistakes, pick myself up, and still savour the unexpected.

To my regret I have a train to catch and cannot stay to see how this might end.

One day I will go back to see the art gallery.

35.

I arrive at the station about two hours before the train is due, but that is common practice in India. The station is spartan, and smells of old stone, but bright blue and yellow rubbish bins deal with the litter. There are sleeping dogs, and rats, but not the desperation of Gorakhpur or Varanasi. (Was that really only three months ago? Am I really writing, without a frisson of horror, about rats running about a railway station? I know there are rats on the stations at home, but we don't often see them.) A security man, in khaki, strolls up and down, waving a long stick; thin women walk along the railway lines, clearing rubbish; the air is heavy, sultry. The metal bench I sit on is extraordinarily hard.

The train arrives and I settle into a sweaty plastic berth, cocoon myself between two sheets and a scratchy blanket, and doze. Three men creep into my cabin in Bangalore; they ignore me and I do not feel alarmed. I couldn't have considered sleeping in a train carriage with three male strangers without a fit of the vapours before I left home. I am being bombarded with evidence that I am becoming a different woman. Though I'm not sure I recognise her on a daily basis yet.

We surface around half past six, ignoring the man-sweat smell and pottering along to metal bowls at the end of the carriage to clean our teeth. Dawn breaks over the suburbs of Chennai. The slums do not surprise me. I am more intrigued by the urban trains, slithering even slower than we are, and with advertisements on their sides – for banks, paint, pressure cookers, condoms!

We crawl into Chennai Central. It is dingy, grimy with the dirt of trains and travellers, but swarms of purposeful people would suggest it is effective. No one would recognise the woman who wanted to shrink back into the airport in Kathmandu. I take a determined route for the pre-paid taxi stand, with a *tuk tuk* driver following, demanding six hundred rupees for the drive to the bus station (my *Lonely Planet* insists it should cost one hundred). I laugh, and slowly the price comes down; I keep walking until he reaches one hundred rupees, and only then do I turn and agree. (Me – haggling, on my own, with a *tuk tuk* driver, without any nerves fluttering in my stomach – even finding it amusing!)

We head into the bustle of Chennai, past new glass-fronted

buildings cheek-by-jowl with heaps of rubbish and the occasional cow; and then he pulls into a garage and demands fifty rupees for fuel: I have no change and refuse – besides I am certain this is a scam, though I can't see how it works. Off again, and now he hurtles through a red traffic light and overtakes in unlikely places; he announces he needs another twenty rupees for the car park at the bus station. No, I insist, we agreed a hundred. The air between us bristles, and – for a moment – my overconfidence fights back. How sensible is it to upset a *tuk tuk* driver when I have no idea where I am? Pride will not allow me to back down. But he could take me anywhere, abandon me to the mercies of anyone. Nobody knows where I am; I could be dumped in the backstreets of Chennai and it would take days – weeks possibly – before the lack of emails home became a cause for concern. My stomach does its flipping thing and I concentrate on stopping my mind imagining my body slumped in an Indian gutter. Not so brave now.

Then, mercifully – and as if by magic – he turns into the bus station. Again he demands another twenty rupees and again I refuse, which is obviously churlish when he has elected not to kidnap me, nor rob me at knifepoint. But the relief of arriving safely has made me arrogant.

And then he surprises me; he strides across the car park to fetch a trolley for my luggage and I give him ten rupees for his trouble; at last, we grin at each other. It is a game we have played, and fought to a draw.

I find the bus for Pondicherry. I cannot climb the ladder and secure my luggage on the roof, but a passenger spots me struggling, offers a helping hand and dissolves into the crowd before I can thank him. I settle myself behind the driver; he has fixed three smoking incense sticks above his sacred picture; I hope it will mask the fact that I haven't washed for twenty-four hours.

36.

Pondicherry is unlike any other city in India. The French, who traded here for centuries, have left a lasting legacy. Of course there are still squalid streets with families huddled under makeshift shelters. The outskirts of the city are overgrown with the customary Indian chaos. But near the sea the solid buildings are painted in Mediterranean cream, flooded with the shock of bougainvillea. The stench of the river is tempered by wafts of jasmine. Catholic churches rub shoulders with Hindu temples. There are crammed bazaars, modern coffee shops and bookshops; there is a glorious concoction of restaurants. Road names – confusingly – are in French and English. Local people speak Tamil, or Telugu, or Malayalam, and Hindi, and French. It is a jubilant, patchwork city.

Temperatures reach a searing forty degrees during the day; like most local people I doze or retreat into air conditioning during the afternoons. But in the early evening the town comes alive. Crowds swarm out of hibernation to meander along the sea wall and savour the salt breeze. They are welcomed by a tide of popcorn and candy floss sellers, traders in sandalwood, coral necklaces, drums, chess sets, and peacock fans; a band trumpets below a solid statue of Gandhi. Families stroll hand in hand; young men jostle and swagger; young women titter; a group of grubby children target the occasional tourist; a few unlikely joggers weave among the crowds.

I love it. For the first time, it is safe for me to be alone in the streets in the evening. I feel like a child let out to play. I have refused to wallow in reminiscences of evenings out in the market town where I live; refused to acknowledge that the need to stay safe is particularly limiting once it gets dark. But there is nothing here to discomfort me; I merge into meandering crowds and am infected by the sheer delight of sea air.

At breakfast one morning my reading is interrupted by Kristen, a willowy Swiss woman who was born in Sri Lanka. She slips into the table beside me and asks directly about my solitary travelling. She is as eager to hear about my journey as I am about hers. She, too, loves Pondicherry; she feels it is the only town in India where she would choose to settle for a month or two. She should know: she has spent the last two years in an agency co-ordinating tsunami relief in Tamil Nadu.

'I am weary of India; they treat each other so badly,' she sighs, her voice laden with disappointment. I'm not sure I want to hear this; I've spent the last couple of months coming to terms with Indian contradictions and am not sure I can open that discussion again. However, I can't let her go without finding out more about her work.

'It's okay,' she says, as if trying to convince herself. 'But if an Indian can make money, he will – it doesn't matter if you are a tourist, or a neighbour. They cheat each other as much as they cheat you. I'll give you an example. I ordered a thirty-five thousand litre water tank – having worked out how much one village would need in an emergency, with each person allotted just two litres of water a day. It was all ordered and paid for; I went to another site for a couple of days and came back to find that the builder had fitted one that was only ten thousand litres. I had to look for him, ask him why, and he shrugged, smirked, then said it will be enough. So I have to complain to everyone, write letters, spend hours on the phone, rant in meetings, and three months later we have a tank the right size. And it has all been like this – we have done good things, but at every step there have been problems.'

She spears her food, months of wrangling expressed in her attack on an unsuspecting omelette.

'They aren't all like this,' I try. 'Some of the people I've met have been very kind. The problem I have is in telling the difference between who might cheat me and who will be helpful.'

'Oh yes, some are kind. But many aren't. And it is impossible to judge quickly. I have lived in India, on and off, for eight years, and I still cannot tell. I just assume they will all cheat me now. Don't forget – even some behaviour that isn't obvious is deliberate – the men who pee in the street in front of you are doing it on purpose, to insult you.'

They seem to pee in front of anyone, but then I think again. 'I did have a man rearrange his genitals in front of me yesterday, but I glared at him and he turned away. All the same, I know India is hard work but there are wonderful aspects to it – and Pondicherry is easier than most places.' I feel as if I am making some sort of apology, fighting a losing corner, but am not sure why.

'India is difficult for everyone,' she continues. 'Tourists who go home and say it's wonderful have gone around with their eyes closed. They see the Taj Mahal, and the forts and palaces, the beaches of Goa, but they never step from their hotels and smell the streets, never step over the broken limbs of beggars, never joke with the *tuk tuk* drivers.' Her omelette is mangled to the point of scrambled eggs by now.

I haven't met such anger before. I'm not sure if I should challenge it, or share it, or somehow pacify her. Though I do know I want to find out as much as I can about how India is for her. What to ask her first?

'So how do you manage – for instance, how do you deal with beggars?', I ask.

'I don't give to beggars,' she begins. 'But I play with the children; most people don't have time for them, but I will stop and play. Nobody seems to play with them – but a few minutes fooling around and giggling with them, that can be fun. Sometimes I give them sweets; but never money – I never give the children money. And it is only sometimes – so they never know if I have sweets, and if they try to rifle my pockets I stop and go away.' I tell her of a child who had slapped me when I refused her money in Jodhpur.

'If they slap me, I slap them back. That was hard at first, but they don't slap me again. I don't hurt them, of course, but they get the message. For some children slapping is the only language they understand.'

Could I ever reach a point where I might slap a child? After all those years working in Child Protection I certainly hope not. I recognise a hint of pedantry, but still cannot believe that a quick slap, a clip round the ear, six of the best, never did anyone any harm. I've seen too many people defend brutality in the name of discipline. No – India hasn't changed me that much; I shall still respond to children with what I hope is compassion.

'But I will give money to the old women,' Kristen relents. Maybe she has interpreted my silence as disapproval. 'I cannot bear to see old women scrabbling in the rubbish. There is no system to help them. The young women – there are other opportunities for them. Most of the beggars are organised; but not the old women – there is nothing for them.'

Our time is running out and I want to know everything.

'So where are you living while you are here?' I ask.

'For three months I have been with an Indian family – they have been kind.' She does not see the incongruity of their kindness and her disenchantment, and I am too curious about domestic life to ask that question.

'So what is life like for the women, at home, in their families?'

'They have affairs.' She grins. 'Parents arrange marriages, and everything is done properly. Then they have affairs. And then they go to the temple to make everything all right.'

There is no time to reply – she has work to do.

I retreat to a coffee shop with my diary. I had not expected to meet anyone able to speak so candidly about the challenges of living here. In just twenty minutes Kristen has run the gauntlet of every Indian contradiction. I feel as if I am wading through thinking-soup. I can't make any sense of the dialogue between India's glorious legends, her economic successes, and the reality of squalor on so many of her streets. After yesterday's euphoria I wallow in self-doubt, again. Maybe I'm the wrong age to be in India: the young can wander into ashrams, lounge around on beaches; and the very old are revered, treasured. While I'm left asking questions with no answers.

Nothing for it; I'll just have to have another cup of tea.

37.

Is it possible that I, too, can find comfort in an ashram? For centuries they have provided spiritual retreat for India's devout. More recently they are also a refuge for westerners seeking escape.

One of the best-known, and wealthiest, ashrams in India is in Pondicherry. The main buildings are sheltered behind a heavy sandstone wall; the solid gate is painted in matching pink. I arrive just as a line of schoolgirls, dressed in deep red and cream, are visiting. I slip in behind them, and am herded along a short concrete path past pots of luxuriant green plants into a central garden, to find a vast frangipani tree (sadly not in fragrant bloom), leaning slightly and supported by sturdy steel girders, chipmunks skittering in its branches. In its shade is the *samadhi*, a chest containing the mortal remains of Sri Aurobindo, the founder of the ashram, and the Mother – a Frenchwoman who joined him. It resembles an altar, decorated with flowers meticulously arranged in pinks and yellows and whites, surrounded by a sea of green leaves. It is a glorious tapestry of flowers – rearranged, I learn, every day.

Pilgrims shuffle barefoot around the *samadhi*; many kneel, bow their heads into the flowers, touch petals with infant tenderness and bring their fingers to their lips. Others nod in reverence, and then line the walls of the quiet courtyard to meditate. I don't know what story underpins their reverence, and maybe it doesn't matter. I have come to discover if peace and quiet are possible in India. I am surprised how much I miss it; maybe Wiltshire has spoiled me. Night noises at home consist of owls hooting and the occasional bark of a muntjac deer. Even in daylight the traffic grumble is little more than a drone.

Most of the visitors are Indian, profoundly moved by their devotions. (These are high caste Indians, in neat suits and glittery saris. There are no grubby *salwar kameez* here, no *lungis* frayed from dragging along the floor, no calloused feet.) Alongside them is a predictable scattering of western hippies (I suppose I have to put myself in this category) with floaty clothes and unreliable hair. Most are much younger than me, with earnest faces, sitting in orthodox yoga poses with expressions full of nothing.

I make my way between them – a few are disturbed by my footfall, open a blurry eye and close it again immediately, as if I am no more significant than a passing breeze. I find a corner, make one feeble attempt at crossing my legs – it used to make my knees ache when I was at school, so there's no hope of me sitting like that for long now – before settling quietly on one buttock. I sink into green silence for a while. I am meant to be meditating.

On what? On the quiet beauty of the courtyard? On the contrasting mayhem of the streets outside? On the mysteries of my journey, that has led me here? My inefficient meditations bring no inspiration, and so I exit via the bookshop and buy a pamphlet exploring the principles of the ashram.

The pamphlet is a collection of the writings of Sri Aurobindo and the Mother. The aim of the ashram, they claim, is to enable members to attain a higher spiritual life, and thus promote the divine on earth.

Yoga, meditation and physical exercise are the foundations of their devotions, the earthly means to their spiritual end. I might be able to manage the yoga, if they allowed me to prop myself against a wall for the tricky poses, and let me off sitting cross-legged. Meditation; it takes practice, I've been told. And exercise – in this heat?

Followers must give up homes, families, lovers. The ashram can countenance no earthly pleasuring: no politics, no drinking, no smoking, no worldly goods, no sex, no falling in love. So – no fun then. Which doesn't make much sense for the young and virile, nor for the likes of me – with less time left to enjoy myself.

I read and reread the pamphlet. I think I'm looking for inspiration, the promised Indian enlightenment. But I am particularly perturbed by the final sections. Members of the ashram are urged to work – in schools, growing food for the community; and yet there is an assumption that they will also be attended by servants who, it is clear, should be treated kindly but without the suggestion that they can place as much as a toe on Sri Aurobindo's spiritual path. An Indian attitude to caste and status has invaded even this ashram without question. Later I hear of a beggar whipped for pausing in the doorway in the hope of scraps of left-over food; he was, apparently, contaminating the ashram.

Nothing ventured; maybe reading will inform my meditations on a second visit, make them more productive. I return to the quiet courtyard, inhale the soft smell of green – such a contrast to the dust and grime of the street – assume a meditative pose and try to concentrate. But my reading has distracted rather than consoled me; I look around: some of the faithful are clearly asleep, others fiddle with their fingers, a few are deep within themselves. The shade of the tree is restorative, but the ashram has disappointed me.

I turn to leave, looking briefly for a toilet before the sanitary desert of the streets. The gents' is easy to find; I ask a guide for mine and am dismissed with a curt, 'Outside!' A woman in a red sari pees in the gutter near the doorway. Presumably the same ethic that assumes the rightful place for servants also prescribes the toileting facilities for women.

38.

Back to Chennai. This is my final stop in India before flying to Singapore. I am weary of my own circular thinking. Will I be sorry to leave? I flop back on my hotel bed, soothed by the grumble of air conditioning. Horns blare in the hot streets outside. The room smells slightly musty, unaired; there is a corner of mould in the bathroom and a wet patch behind the toilet that I refuse to think about.

I stand to look out of the dusty window. Traffic is motionless on the road outside. Beyond that, the river, black and sluggish, meanders through the city. Five shacks are perched on its banks – surely they will be washed away when the monsoons come? Three men squat to defecate by the river; a few feet away children are playing cricket with sticks and a small stone. I can't see any women from here.

It is time to read through my diaries.

I am no longer horrified by India. The stink and chaos of Gorakhpur, which had sent me scampering to Tika for comfort, seems a long time ago. My stomach still knots as I hold my gaze above the limbless beggars, but my conscience no longer eats at me in the hot nights. I can greet persistent, even aggressive, *tuk tuk* drivers with humour now. I lie about my family life without a second thought. I negotiate the realities of the street without alarm.

So – I can manage myself here. That does not mean that it has been easy. Organising myself as a woman alone has been hard work. I have rarely felt unsafe, except perhaps in the *tuk tuk* last time I was in Chennai. Let's not go over that again. Though it is a brutal reminder that I have needed to pay more attention to issues of risk in India than in any other country I have visited. Pondicherry and Goa are the only places to see me walking alone in the evening streets, and even then I have been scrupulous about retreating into the hotel before ten. (But then – how many English cities are safe for lone women at night? Maybe I have grown complacent in Wiltshire.)

And maybe I am protected, just a little, by my age. While there are hints that a western cult of youth is beginning to invade India, particularly the shops of Bangalore, respect for age and the aging is embedded in the complex culture. My gender and skin colour make me visible; but wrinkles carry their own advantages. Nevertheless, I need some distance between myself and the effort of managing here on my own. I'm weary. And so, no, I will not be sorry to leave.

Will I come back? That's an even more difficult question. Right now, from the isolation of a hotel room, I think not. But I know myself well enough to know that, within weeks of leaving, I'll wonder about the mountains of Assam or the hot streets of Kolkata. And, in spite of all the hassles, I will want to go there on my own.

Three months in India has, at times, felt like a long time. In three days I shall head for Singapore. I have been assured that the contrast with India will astound me. Bring it on.

39.

My last day. Two days ago I spent the evening with Vedesh, on a brief visit to Chennai, and another cousin, Kalanath. He is a quiet man, who sips a slow beer and says little as Vedesh talks of a friend who has bought him a bottle of Scotch on the basis of his knowing a professor from Oxford. Vedesh must return to Mumbai; and Kalanath invites me to spend my last day – a Sunday – with his family.

He arrives, as agreed, at eleven. His daughter Shirina, aged eight, clambers around the car, giving me sidelong glances and shouting instructions to her father regarding where we should go next. He drives past solid colonial buildings, and then along the beach where families are unravelling picnics and boys playing cricket with a stone ball. Kalanath came here as a child; he, too, played cricket here. We chat about

England's lamentable performance in Australia, tiptoe around India's lack of success in the World Cup. Shirina, not to be outdone, tells me that she loves school, and that her best subject is drawing. Somehow the three of us negotiate a conversation that hovers between cricket and drawing; we are already friends.

We drive out into the suburbs, stopping to collect Kalanath's aunt and uncle; he has recently undergone an appendectomy and slides gingerly into the front of the car. His aunt is an elegant woman, in her sixties, with lush hair and an orange and green sari that sparkles in the sunlight. She sits beside me, smelling of something luxuriously eastern, and asks immediately about my journey, where I have been. I try to explain that I am not only interested in buildings, but in how people live their lives.

'I should think that must be uncomfortable at times,' she replies.

I am caught off-guard by her unexpected empathy. I flash what I hope is a smile of gratitude at her insight before she and Kalanath are rattling away in Telugu. This, they tell me, is a local language, rarely spoken now, and the subject of her PhD. I long to know more; the aunt and I have age and education in common and I sense a mutual curiosity; but we have arrived at Kalanath's flat and my questions are lost.

He opens the door with the pride of a child with a new bike. This is a recent, longed-for, investment. He and his wife, Mehal, have painted the sitting room in white, one bedroom in red, and another a deep blue. The galley kitchen is alive with steam from simmering rice and wafts of spices, and beyond a tiny washroom tumbles with a washing machine. There is a small *puja* corner, crammed with imagery and a small offering of rice. This is Kalanath's home, his world, his pride and joy.

Mehal greets me, then perches on the edge of a seat.

'You are hungry, auntie? You are thirsty, auntie? We have tea? Water? You need the bathroom, auntie?' I search for a way to interrupt her subservience. Her urgency softens when I bring out my photographs; we look at them together as mothers.

I have no idea why I feel no need to fib here. I admit to being widowed, to wanting to travel before the years take over. There is something about this generous family that makes honesty possible.

'Here it is hard for widows, auntie. They cannot go out, cannot travel like you do. And if there is no one to look after them, well . . .' The sentence is never finished; I know that begging is often the only solution for a widow with no brother or brother-in-law to turn to.

'It is different in England?' How can I begin to describe the differences? Widowhood in Britain can be a challenge, but at least it doesn't destroy all choices. They are as bewildered by the idea that a woman might choose to live alone as I am at the thought of having no alternative but to find another man to care for me. Oddly, we are united in our shared lack of understanding. I feel neither patronised nor dismissed. I am not invisible, as happens so often at home, even though my ideas and experiences are so alien to them.

Their kindness nurtures me. I share their Sunday meal: basmati rice with a creamed vegetable curry. My lips sting from the spices; Kalanath quietly refills my water and ignores my streaming eyes. The discomfort is worth it – this is almost up to Chandresh's standard. Family chat, in sundry languages (rarely English) drifts around me. Afterwards Shirina draws me a tiny picture of Hanuman, the monkey god, that will fit snugly inside my purse. He will, they promise me, sort out any problems along my way.

There are hugs when I leave, and assurance that I must stay with them if I return. My eyes prickle with their generosity.

Kalanath tries to explain the family history as we drive away, but I lose track of cousins and sisters and especially aunts.

'We are going to see Anita (the mother of my colleague); she is my mother's sister. It was hard for her, too, when we were children. Her husband – he is here now, but when we were small he was away. She had to bring up the two girls alone.'

My colleagues' parents and sister stand to attention in their sitting room to welcome me. It is a small, ill-lit room (the lack of light helps to keep it cool), with one sofa and a couple of less comfortable chairs where the women perch. The air smells lightly stale, as if the room is kept for best. Kalanath slinks into a corner, leaving me with the centre stage. I share my photographs.

'You must be so proud of your daughter,' I tell them. 'She is a good doctor, and so kind. I loved working with her.' (This is easy to say – it is true!)

They preen, then ask, 'We hear you are a professor at Oxford?'

'No; that is one of Vedesh's ideas.' I catch a sharing of grins and grimaces; no one seems surprised and nothing more is said. The women head for the kitchen to fetch more cake.

'How have you found India?' asks Sri's father. I try to explain how confusing it has been at times. But his question was merely a polite preamble; he reaches for a book and Kalanath sighs: he has seen this before.

'Read this; you will see that there is nothing new in history. Everything has happened before.' He has rewritten the *Mahabharata* in iambic pentameter. He points me to ancient invasions that mirror the situation in Iraq to prove the inevitability of history. He seems to be suggesting that, given the unchanging nature of behaviour, humankind cannot avoid the repetition of past mistakes. My determination to avoid talking about politics is wavering.

'The poetry; this is written like Shakespeare.' I try to deflect him.

'Well, you must copy the best. Shakespeare is the best. And then you can use the best to tell the best stories. See here – ' and he stabs at another bellicose passage. It seems I am not permitted to remain neutral. The women have returned and I want to include them.

'I take your point,' I concede, 'about history being repeated. But I don't agree that there is nothing we can do to change that.'

There is a hiss of breath from the women; disagreement is rare here. But I've started so I'll finish. 'If women ran the world, they might make different decisions.'

Kalanath brings his book in front of his face; I cannot tell if he is laughing or simply wishes to keep out of the conversation.

'Women cannot take high office;' – the father's voice is rising – 'for one week every month they cannot be in office. They cannot go to meetings. And so they cannot hold power. In traditional homes there are extra rooms for women when menstruating.'

'But India had one of the first women prime ministers in the world!'

'Precisely.' He is triumphant. 'You can see why it does not work.'

I concede that his knowledge of Indian history is far greater than mine. I dare not mention Margaret Thatcher. But still I cannot let this go. In spite of the women's discomfort, Kalanath's giggling, and Sri's father's surprise, I am enjoying myself.

'Nevertheless, women approach things differently.' Anita crashes her teacup. 'If there is a problem,' I persist, 'women drink tea and talk about it; there would be much less fighting.' I have a ridiculous image of international negotiations regarding the relative merits of Earl Grey and Lapsang Souchong, but decide to keep that to myself.

'I agree, women are not the same.' Pardon? He repeats himself. Is he really seeing a different point of view?

'So if women were in power we might drink gallons of tea but have fewer wars?'

At last he grins; the women sink back in their seats. Kalanath peers from behind his book; I dare not catch his eye as it will set us both off.

It is time to leave. There are more hugs, more invitations. When I woke this morning I was ready to leave India. I have spent a day wallowing in her generosity; Kalanath and Mehal ring in the evening and repeat their invitation to return and stay with them.

Indian contradictions have finally defeated me.

PART SIX

WAITING IN MALAYSIA

40.

Singapore. I arrive (three strands of tinsel still glittering) with the stench of Indian chaos in my nostrils, to be met with streets that might be brushed with *Flash* every morning. I knew there would be no cows, but where is the litter? The empty crisp packets? The newspaper smelling of chips? What do the young do with their chewing gum? Eating in the street, I soon learn, is not allowed.

Though there is no need; Singapore is food heaven. (I am a dreadful cook, as my daughters will testify. But I love good food.) There are elegant restaurants, where world cuisine dinners are served on graceful plates; there are hawker centres – removed from the streets but still smelling of frying, and selling cheap, delicious local food; there are back-street restaurants from Italy, Lebanon, Morocco; there are platters from every corner of Asia. (How does MacDonald's make money here, when there are so many wonderful alternatives to choose from?) Elegant cafés tempt me with healthy sandwiches and the bitter smell of coffee. There are so many that, on my first day, I suffer an existential crisis trying to decide where to buy my cappuccino.

Restaurants are there to feed shoppers. Food – I understand the joy of food, but have never quite understood the passion for shopping. Sssss – I am well aware of a collective female hissing; I am letting the side down, admitting that I find shopping, as a leisure activity, tedious. I pass infinite, immaculate stores with contributions from Gucci and Louis Vuitton; malls teeming with stalls selling glittering costume jewellery, snowstorm Buddhas, watches, mobile phones, cameras, DVDs, handbags, fabrics; small shops with a single dress in their windows; vast suppliers of everything from washing machines to garden equipment to nuts and bolts. It's all too much; I must find another café; drink tea.

Night falls, and still the streets are busy. I could stroll safely at midnight if I had the energy. Nobody takes any notice of me. And not only because I am dressed in the cloak of invisibility here. Everyone is far too busy shopping. It is the leisure activity of choice. It has fuelled the economic success of Singapore; the island has transformed from post-war squalor and poverty into its current prosperity by persuading as many as possible to spend as much money as possible buying as many clothes, plasma-screened televisions, PCs, laptops, DVD players, home music centres, washing machines, swimming pools, hot tubs, plants, crockery, jewellery ... Where do they put all this stuff? And what do they do with all the stuff they must get rid of to make space for the new stuff they buy?

I don't understand shopping. Well, I understand the need to buy things to keep alive, clothed and occasionally entertained. But given the choice between settling on the sofa with a book or meandering in shops – well, there is no contest.

Still, shopping is what everyone does here. My not liking shops is a pathetic excuse for failing to experiment with Singapore's most popular leisure activity. And I try. I stroll through stores heady with perfume spray, past women with identical make-up and identical smiles. I need toothpaste; it takes over half an hour to find a pharmacy in the far corner of a mall, and almost as long to find my way out. I try again. I explore plazas overflowing with trinkets. I linger among stylish furniture, admire perfect plates. My feet ache, in spite of my sensible shoes. I retreat to a café (when I can choose one) with my book.

What can I possibly need? I tip out the contents of my rucksack, trying to discover if there is something missing that I might like to buy. Two floaty shirts, one t-shirt, two floaty skirts, one pair of trousers, underwear. Toiletries: enough to keep me clean. The appearance of fine lines did not trouble me at home and I certainly feel no need for expensive creams here. First aid kit. An MP3 player: music for bus trips. Mobile phone. Guidebook. Novel (swapped in hostels). My one indulgence: a radio with short wave, crackly access to the BBC World Service. No, there is nothing else that I need.

I do, I know, miss the point of Singapore.

However, there are compensations. For three days I flourish in sterile invisibility. Nobody stares at me, questions me, strokes my arms, tries to bamboozle me into a *tuk tuk*. I can do exactly as I please, safely.

The perfections of Singapore are typified on the island of Sentosa, a beach haven just off the south coast. Enticements for tourists begin at the station, with its gaggle of eateries, one soothes by South-American rhythms, a second energised by a brass band. Fans whirr, rotating stifling air. A stiff breeze appears from nowhere and an orchestra of paper cups flies across the courtyard, followed by an urgency of waiters trying to collect them all. Peace is restored in seconds.

There is too much to see in one visit. I could 'encounter' primates, snakes, parrots: I think this is some sort of display, not an encounter of the close kind. I could wander among tropical butterflies. Dolphins are already lining up to entertain me. I could explore an aquarium, with its touch pool and underwater tunnels. There is a suggestion I have always wondered about the texture of baby-shark skin; they don't know me very well. But explore it I do, even take a few photographs of turtles and dogfish – and of a hologram of a shark threatening to swallow me whole. (It is a competent photograph. But holograms are images that do not exist. How does that work?)

Not interested in animals? I could climb inside a replica of Singapore's Merlion, wander at a panoramic view, watch animations of sea dragons and mermaids. The sky tower might carry me even higher. But I have already swung across in the cable car and feel no need for greater heights.

More interested in history? There is the Images of Singapore museum, with its dash through the multi-ethnic excitements of the island. Or a coastal fort with memorabilia from World War II, with life-sized replicas to complete the picture. Too tame? There is a trapeze for the intrepid, luge for the adrenalin-fuelled, golf for the sedate. But we are not expected to walk from one delight to the next: blue buses, always running on time, propel us round the island. Or there are three choreographed nature trails; I try one and challenge their definition of 'nature.'

So much to see. So much to do. All, of course, for the young and active. No quiet corners for women whose idea of joy is a peaceful corner to read a book. Somehow I propel myself round, though I'm not sure why. It is not like me to be so conforming.

After five hours I have had enough. Families, I can see, are still racing from one excitement to another; children tug on parental arms in the urgency of their delights. I don't think it's simply my age that slows me down, though it does. I want time to take it all in. My solution is to make for a beach, to read, write in my diary. The sand, soft and fine, could have been sifted its grains are so regular. Palm trees line the pathway at precise intervals. There are no plastic bottles bobbing in the water, no rancid stink of seaweed. Young men play beach volleyball, careful lest they stray beyond the definitions of their court; there is none of the fucking language that I heard on the beach at Manly. Children potter in quiet waves without shrieking. The setting sun bathes Sentosa in pink; and I feel somewhat churlish questioning such perfection.

I head for an evening display. As I sit scribbling in my diary, waiting for the entertainment to begin, my neighbour interrupts to ask how I am enjoying Singapore.

'It is unusual,' I reply, carefully. 'Everything is so well-organised. Everyone conforms, does what they are expected to do. There is nothing out of place.'

'Everything is where God wants it to be,' he replies, with a sage nod of his head. Surely Mammon has played a significant part? But the bravado that led me to question Sri's father feels out of place here. I might be invisible, but still – I must conform.

On my way home I pass the only graffito on the island: PUNK IS RESISTANCE. I want to stand beside it and cheer. But I suspect the culprit was sent to bed without his supper long ago, and now obeys the rules, just like the rest of us.

41.

Where to now? After the chaos of India the predictability of Singapore is, briefly, reassuring. But, within days, I am bored. Not only because I am bored with shopping – I have wandered into a museum or two, taken a boat down the river, investigated Eastern art. But Singapore lacks excitement.

Apparently, sometime before the War, before his lips grew thin with paternal disapproval, my father was thrown out of Raffles in Singapore for sliding down the banisters. It is an elegant colonial building; the flunkey in reception stands to attention the minute I walk in; Maggie Smith should be holding court in the dining room wearing a long frock and gloves. The banisters are wooden, polished, tempting. What if ... but I can only dream of the excitement of sliding down them. My father's behaviour could be dismissed as the high jinks of a young man; he probably raced up the stairs, two at a time, threw his leg over the wooden rail and 'whee'd' all the way down. While I would plod up, holding the wretched banister for balance; and then what – hitch up my skirt? Fling my leg behind me, as if getting on a horse? My flinging days are long gone.

Even so, I need to tell someone.

'My father,' I begin, to the flunkey on reception. He does not look at me; nor smile; nor even nod to show that he has heard what I've said. There is nothing in his flunkey manual to help him deal with the fantasies of middle-aged women. I retaliate by using the toilet and leaving a gold-plated tap running. It is the only act of defiance that seems remotely possible.

I can't stay here long. I want to press north, into Malaysia, head for the beaches of Thailand. But – at home – life has become more complicated in my absence. Tessa is no longer going to deliver her baby in Caracas; she is home – to make sure he has the security of a British passport.

We speak on the phone; she is solidly patient, tolerant of her bulk and already nurturing her baby. I can picture her, her fingers resting beneath her breasts and stroking a tiny skull beneath her fingers. Her bump will smell of creams and talcum powder.

I want to put one hand round her shoulders and another on her tummy, to feel the baby-kicks of my grandson. I want to feed her tea and oranges that come all the way from China. I begin to ration the times I can check my phone for texts from her. I wish someone would email me a photo – I need to see what she looks like with a bump. I need to go home, just for a while, to welcome this new person for myself.

But not yet. I have planned a year. My round-the-world ticket, while negotiable, is my right to roam.

I am, of course, beset with an internal dialogue.

'What sort of mother are you, staying so far away, when your daughter is having her first baby? You should be there, reassuring, knitting, taking her to *Mothercare* to buy nappies.'

'Yes, but – she is well cared-for; she is staying with her dad; she has sisters around her. She will only be at home for six weeks after the baby arrives – then she'll go back to Caracas. And this is my Gap Year – planned, longed-for; I can't just give up, go home, be a grandmother, as if this doesn't matter.' I flick through the diaries, try to spot the moment when my initial inquiry as to whether I was capable of such wandering became a lust for it, but cannot find it. I am almost unable to recognise myself as the woman who left home.

I fight with myself at night; there are no right answers. But what surprises me – although not my daughters – is just how much I want to carry on travelling. I've made it this far; survived India; I have a plan to explore the Far East, go north into China, take the trans-Siberian railway to Moscow and fly home from there. I'm living my Dream – I can't give it up, not now, not even for a baby.

Well, maybe for a week. I'll go home for a week.

These are contradictory, aching, waiting days.

42.

There can be no better place to wait than Melaka. The bus has driven through palm groves, gentle hills, tropical forests. Air conditioning protects me from the humidity, but the rich green alone is evidence of hot wetness.

More striking, after India, is the sparse population: there are a few isolated bungalows, passing cows and water buffalo, men in wide-brimmed hats working in fields. The space entices me; but I must not set off alone here; there are seriously wild animals in these beautiful hills.

I have no idea what to expect in Melaka. My first delight is the hotel; situated in a shabby street in Chinatown, the owners have converted an old shophouse into an original guesthouse. The building was commissioned by the Dutch, at a time when home-owners were taxed according to the size of the fronts of their houses. The result: a narrow frontage, and behind that a series of three airwells creating three internal courtyards, each with balcony and interconnecting floors above. The design was made even more unusual by the Chinese builders, who ignored many of the Dutch instructions and introduced dragons and fountains – excellent feng shui!

I glean much of this information from Miss Jo, a Punjabi cleaner at the hotel. We strike up a conversation while she is dusting the bookshelves around the first courtyard; by the time we realise we share a name we are the best of friends. It is a friendship of women; we are both eager to talk about our families, our stories. To an outsider it might look like gossip.

'Where did you learn to speak such good English?' What I really want to know how someone so knowledgeable ends up cleaning.

'I am sixty-seven,' she replies. 'I speak Punjabi and Malay and English, and a little French and Mandarin. I worked for the stock exchange, but there are no other opportunities for me now. They tell me I am too old. I have no money, so I must work. But my son, he stays with an aunt in London; he will do well there. There are better opportunities for him there.'

She preens as she talks of him, but my questions are curtailed by a scowl from the woman behind the reception desk. Miss Jo scuttles back to work.

Five minutes later she is back, muttering, with furtive glances over her shoulder.

'You must come to the Sikh New Year; you are my guest; on Thursday.'

We agree a time and place to meet, and she is gone, leaving me wondering what I have let myself in for. Should I bring a gift? Do I need to dress up (as if I have anything smart enough to look like dressing up)?

Thursday comes, and I make my way, empty-handed but in a freshly-washed skirt, through Little India, with its unmistakable spice-smells, to the Sikh temple. The entrance is through an archway painted in greens and yellows and purple, leading to a scorched courtyard and dark temple, its interior filled with shadowy figures.

I pause in the doorway; do I walk in? Wait here? Miss Jo has pre-empted me. A young man, in a long blue robe over his grey trousers, comes out to greet me. I explain that I am expected.

'I know.' His words are terse, but the tone is kind.

He gently drapes a scarf across my head, reminds me to leave my shoes, then nudges me into the temple. From the outside it had looked dark, but in here it is bright, sun gleaming through windows and echoed in gold on the walls and the glorious colours of the robes. I can smell people, and incense. Men sit, crossed-legged on the left-hand side of the temple, women and children on the right. Ahead is an altar, draped in a gold cloth, with a priest behind it, chanting and waving what looks to me like a wand with a tail of goat's hair. Two musicians sit to one side. I drop to the floor on the women's side.

Miss Jo is behind the altar as I go in, looking so different in her pink and white *salwar kameez* and head cover. But soon her offices are over and she sits beside me, whispering explanations as the celebrations continue.

I am the only white person there; but don't feel conspicuous, as I had in India. I manage to sit cross-legged for about half an hour. Which is a record; even at school, under the proprietary scowl of Miss Bloss, I couldn't do that. The wooden floor gets harder with each passing minute and I resort to buttock-shuffling for another hour until we stand up.

There is music and chanting. Then a pause, and the priest, in a thin white robe, long white beard and a voice to melt chocolate, tells the story of the festival; Miss Jo explains later that they are remembering five martyrs who refused to cut their hair and convert to Islam. I understand nothing at all, but he could read the phone book and I would still listen all day.

There is a change of tone after the story is told. Notices –

about yoga classes and a cultural programme – are given in English. There is a short prize-giving, gifts for young people who had done well at school, complete with proud parents and photographs. There is more chatting, voices eager now they are released from the gravity of ritual. I massage the pins and needles that have taken over my toes and struggle to my feet, assuming that the celebrations are over. But Miss Jo has grabbed my arm and is tugging me towards a small door behind the altar.

'You must come to lunch.' Miss Jo leads me into a huge hall at the back of the temple, already teeming with families. Tables are laid; people are eating.

'Come – it is busy. I will show you round first.' She has all the excitement of a child showing a new playmate around her house. I am a willing playmate; I remember Wendy houses.

She takes me upstairs, where a row of simple guest rooms offer space for travellers to meditate and study; behind them is a second temple – a vacant space smelling of paint and in the process of being redecorated. Downstairs, we cross a courtyard to a third temple where a bearded priest bows his head and gently wishes me well. I am carried on such an unexpected tide I can only mumble thanks as we return to the food fray.

We look for a place at a long trestle table; two women shuffle up to give us space beside them. Miss Jo seems to settle, but bobs up again, as a man deals out our plastic plates like cards, to find me a spoon. (How did she know that I would fail the eating-rice-with-my-fingers test?) Then one man after another passes by dishing out heaps of rice, dahl, vegetables, curry, yogurt, and – just as I think I can eat no more – sweets and grapes.

The hall is simmering with the smell of curry and euphoric with chatter. I understand nothing but am humbled to be there. Occasionally someone engages in the 'what is your name?' routine, and Miss Jo swells with the coincidence of our names. But it seems that there are few people with her linguistic skills and conversations are limited. It doesn't matter. I am embraced by this Sikh community with all the affection and assurance of family. Which is opportune, when my own thoughts of family feel more urgent by the minute.

As people begin to drift away I ask Miss Jo who I should thank for making me so welcome.

'Only God,' she replies.

We arrange to meet the next day for the cultural programme – there will, I am assured, be music and dancing. But the temple is silent and empty when I arrive. There seems to be some sort of meeting that I do not interrupt, but no sign of entertainment. I lean in the shade of the wall for a while and am about to leave when Miss Jo scurries up.

'No cultural programme, I am sorry, it is cancelled.' She reaches for my hand. 'Come to yoga.'

Curiosity deserts me. Suddenly I cannot face trying to contort my middle-aged body in the company of lithe Asian women. I am stiff from yesterday's cross-legged sitting. I stand no hope of posing like a tree, nor a lion; even welcoming the sun would be a challenge with all that getting up and down. I endure a tsunami of Western reticence, an inability to risk exposing myself, a longing for the invisibility of home. I shake her hand and retreat to the hotel.

You fool – is a little embarrassment really so dreadful?

43.

I met Mark and Kyong Soon on the bus from Singapore. We shared a taxi from the bus station and explored the town together. They are in their early thirties, and it feels odd that they should be interested in me. I am not used to all this attention.

Though, as I come to realise, talking with me means they do not have to talk to each other.

Kyong Soon, from Korea, is in charge of food. Although pale, almost fragile in appearance, her appetite is legendary. It is important to her that we eat well – not as the tourists eat, but in back-street restaurants and hawker centres. For our first supper, she orders three bowls of rice, two plates of fish, two of vegetables and one of tofu. We sit at a plastic table on a street corner, tropical clouds lowering, the sweetest of food-smells steaming from the kitchen and the hubbub of conversation around us. Mark and I manage half of it between us; Kyong Soon is still hungry and talks about pudding. Why isn't she fat?

Mark and I talk as she eats. He is a tall, lean Englishman, brought up in the Far East where his father was in the Services. He has worked, he assures me, for the United Nations, and in earthquake sciences, but is currently trying to secure some sort of 'deal' in Singapore. (Our conversation is, indeed, punctuated with phone calls; he straightens to receive them, stiffens his shoulders as if wearing an imaginary suit.) For a while I wonder if I have stumbled up against another Victor, as his plans seem so unsubstantial. But there is a gentleness about him that I warm to.

And he loves Kyong Soon. She is hungry; we must eat. She is thirsty; we must drink. She wants new shoes; she has new shoes. His devotion could be irritating, but it doesn't feel like that. I have a sense of a man working with every cell of himself to make her happy.

It is so hard for her to be happy – not because she does not love him, but because their transitory lifestyle leaves her floundering. She does, eventually, talk about herself.

'I miss Korea,' she says with such stark simplicity that I have to swallow tears. I understand missing home. 'I come from an island, a small island. I miss my family, my friends. We go back, but it is not the same.'

'When we retire,' Mark promises, 'we will go back. We will live there. You have given up these years to travel with me; you will have your turn.'

'In my language, there is no word for "my". We talk of "our" house, "our" grandmother. I still think of "our" family; it is part of me. And yet I have been away; I am different now. They see me as different.'

How could she not be different? But, while my daughters follow my adventures with enthusiasm (real or feigned, it feels like enthusiasm to me), knowing I shall bounce back into their lives at the end of my year, and with an acknowledgement I will have changed, Kyong Soon's family can only watch her drift further and further away from them.

'I know I could become British,' she continues. 'We have been married for long enough. We have the papers. But then you invaded Iraq. Now I cannot become British; I cannot swear allegiance to a country that does that. So I do not belong anywhere now.'

Mark is restless. I suspect this is an old conversation, one that he has no idea how to resolve. Kyong Soon's distress is palpable and I am tempted to drag up my old counselling skills.

Mark cannot help her bear it; he changes the subject.

'Kyong Soon, you must make sure I don't eat chillies tomorrow. I have a stomach problem,' he explains to me, 'and if it becomes too acid it damages my throat. I can feel it now – I ought to be talking less.'

'So Kyong Soon has to make sure you don't eat chillies?'

'Yes.' Mark seems surprised by the question.

'Can't you do that for yourself?'

There is a fractured moment; I have touched something painful but we defuse the situation with grins and another consultation with the guidebook. I had thought I could see both sides of their difficulties until he said that.

We arrange to meet for supper on their last night in Melaka. They are late arriving and cannot look at each other. I am beginning to feel like a marriage guidance counsellor.

Two beers later, and the cracks split open.

'I cannot bear it,' Kyong Soon cries, 'when his mother

phones. Every week she phones and always he must speak to her. She wants to see him; all the time she wants to see him. But she will not speak to me. I am Korean so I am nothing to her. I will not see them, and cannot bear it when he sucks up to them.'

'It's not as simple as that.' The more Mark reaches out to her, the more she shrugs him off. It seems that the loss of connection with her own family (who do not use mobile phones or internet technologies) feeds her resentment of any evidence of affection from his.

'I can't go on like this. I will go home to Korea, to my family. I can't be with a family who do not want me.' He squirms but cannot satisfy her; her rage eventually subsides. He, a rootless man, has uprooted her, and they have yet to shape a way of being contented together.

They make me feel like a mother, adjudicating in their disputes. They draw me into their misery, and I go willingly – when they can forget their differences they are generous with their time and their humour.

Or maybe it's just that motherhood is on my mind at the moment. It won't be long before I am home.

44.

North to Kuala Lumpur (KL) for the final baby-waiting days. I suppose these aren't the best circumstances in which to explore a new city. My hand is bonded with my phone, alert for every text. Do I rush home today? Tomorrow? How did I ever imagine I would be able to carry on travelling while she was at home giving birth? Finally Tessa is given an induction day; I book my flight. In four days I will return to Singapore and head for Heathrow.

In spite of my distraction, KL is a shock. Where is the cleanliness of Singapore? The space and gentility of Melaka? I arrive late in the afternoon; the streets are dowdy, choking with traffic and sultry tropical air. The bus station is dingy, swarming with people and mysterious signs. I was accustomed to chaos in India, became adept and negotiating it. This is different; it looks as if there should be logic; traffic lights work and road markings are clear, but the engine din and horde of people make me doubt it. I can taste diesel fumes.

Even my hostel alarms me. I bump into a young man in the doorway who tells me, with some surprise, that the lift is working. (Phew – while I'm able to lug my rucksack up a flight of stairs, it still makes me puff.) The lift spits me out on a narrow landing and I am directed through double doors into a large lounge that smells of beer and cigarettes. Young people loaf on sofas, deafened by a DVD; a few sit on green plastic chairs around the tables, smoking; there are more sofas and another TV in the corner. A dark-skinned man at the reception desk greets me with smiles, gives me a key, and directs me beyond the DVD watchers to corner stairs and the bedrooms. Room 415.

It has everything I need – a bed, with bottom sheet and pillow, in pale blue, and a small dressing table. The walls are almost white, smeared with who knows what. The floor has been swept. Mould creeps in the corner; there is a smell of *Germolene*. The light is stark, bright, fluorescent. No top sheet. No window. This is budget living in a big city.

I slump on the bed. How can I sleep in a room that feels like a cupboard, a cell? It might be fine for the young people downstairs, but surely I'm too old for such discomforts now? I want to leave. I hate the room, the hostel, KL.

Take a deep breath. The toilets and showers are close by and clean. I can lock my door. I am safe; I remind myself that is always my priority. The welcome, as promised, was generous. It's cheap and convenient. It is close to the bus station – and I will be catching an early bus back to Singapore. Do I really want to pack myself up, heave my rucksack around these teeming streets to somewhere more salubrious?

I flirt with the idea of two days on the coast, even ring a hotel or two, but they are full. I must distract myself as best I can.

I wouldn't say I ever like the hostel. No – I must be more specific. I never forgive my room for its lack of windows. These cheap rooms are common in the Far East; some people must live in them. My expectations have spoiled me. I have grown used to waking as the dawn edges its pink light into my windows, wafting scented breezes through my curtains. Here, I cannot tell when it is morning. My room – without the light on – is always dark.

I spend some of my time in the lounge, with young men who have not quite got used to their manly bodies, draping limbs over the backs and arms of chairs as if they can think of nothing else to do with them. Most are European – British, Dutch, German. They seem to fill their days with flopping about, and evenings with drinking. I can't work out why they have travelled across the world. Beer cans are scattered on a low table and across the floor. They take little notice of me, – or of each other. The television, with its DVD player, mesmerises them. They watch, of course, films of brutal violence and bonking. And then they are stunned into silence by *The Chronicles of Narnia*. Now I can see why their mothers love them.

There are, naturally, forgiving corners in KL. I negotiate the gleaming new metro. I admire the glass magnificence of the Petronas Towers, but am not tempted to explore them. City views are beginning to blur. I compare the sterility of an air-conditioned shopping mall, which could be almost anywhere in the world, with the night market in Chinatown – brimming with bags and belts and perfume. A man dabs my arm with what he claims to be *Chanel No 5*, but does not take offence when I laugh. I am offered three watches for a hundred ringgits (why would I want three?).

There are museum days; I try to concentrate on stories of

the Orang Asti – an Aboriginal people who live in the Malaysian jungle. I am intrigued with the ceremonial importance of circumcision in Malay culture: princes are carried to the ceremony on a huge model ostrich, covered in blues and reds and greens; the surgeon wields his scissors in public, followed by cheering and parties. Other little boys line up, snip, snip, snip, and then lie side by side, blankets held up in little tents above their tender parts, to recover. I think of my almost-grandson and cross my legs.

My heart is at home. Days fill and pass. I am on the bus. I check in at the airport. Tessa is wheeled into the delivery suite as I climb the steps into the plane. While she and the baby are screaming his way into the world I am somewhere over the Himalayas watching *Easy Rider*. By the time I stop over in Amsterdam I am a grandmother.

PART SEVEN

BABY DAYS

45.

This is not a book about babies. But my journey is punctuated by this week in Wiltshire, and it gives a different meaning to the weeks that follow.

I am at home here. Nothing much has changed in the seven months I've been away. I can find my way down the High Street without recourse to a map. The fruit and veg man in the market still sells bowls of bananas for £1. I dare to read *The Guardian*. Doors are flung open in welcome, arms wrapped round me and I am swung from the floor in the rapture of greetings. I have stories; they have stories. There is too much to say, but we try. Our voices are hoarse with talking; we croak long into the night.

'What will you eat?' Anna asks, expecting, I suspect, an exotic suggestion consisting of bean shoots and lemongrass.

'What I've really missed is jacket potato and cheese!' I can smell it already. She is appalled, her culinary skills spurned. But, dutifully, she fluffs a potato, drips it with butter and a heap of cheese: a feast. Even Chandresh did not cook jacket potato with cheese.

And the baby. I am, of course, besotted. He has big hands and feet, skin slightly wrinkled, like he's been in the bath for hours. He has not, yet, acquired a milky, vomity baby smell, but no doubt that will come. We play genetic jigsaws (does he have his father's eyes? his mother's nose?); within a week he defies us all and becomes uniquely Christopher. One day he will sprout facial hair and use the f-word just to upset his mother (he has already tried peeing up a wall) but for now he is delicious: a contented baby most of the time, getting the hang of the feeding/sleeping/being-awake idea.

Just as nobody prepares one for motherhood, grandmotherhood also comes as a surprise. He brings a deep and powerful joy, beginning somewhere near my toes and erupting from time to time in an urge to kiss the down on his head.

I spend most of the week with Tessa and the baby as they ease into some sort of understanding of themselves and their new place in the world. The days blur into the preoccupations of infancy; life revolves around feeds and nappies, the need for sleep and the realities of food. It is a strange hiatus for me. The unrealities of travelling, unknown hotel rooms and dusty streets, the excitement and the tedium and the alarms, all feel a thousand miles away. I am a bystander in the mother-and-baby cocoon, just for a week - and it is wonderful.

And yet I leave. How can I? Any practical problems (like the tenant living in my house, the unused flights on my round-the-world ticket) are easily overcome. I am left in no doubt that my daughters are pleased to see me. The baby is as enticing as a new lover.

But my journey is not over. I knew, before I came home, I would go back, though nothing alarming will happen if I change my mind and stay. Given the lure of a baby I will not even lose face. But the dreams persist: as the baby sleeps I am buried in a *Lonely Planet* wondering where to go next. I am not ready to put my passport to bed and consume nothing but the delights of grandparenthood.

To their credit, my daughters do not pressure me to stay. Even Tessa – enraptured as she is with milky preoccupations – knows that I will leave. And she will, in a matter of weeks, return with the baby to his South American family.

This does not mean it is easy. I have only three strands of tinsel, ragged now, left on my rucksack. There are, of course, tears. I stand in the departure lounge at Heathrow, ignoring the bleep of buggies for the disabled and the sickly smell of perfumes, and weep. I have never felt the tug of opposites as keenly. This question will never have a right answer.

PART EIGHT

BALMY DAYS

46.

I have two mindless days in Singapore before heading northwards. My pre-baby angst has only heightened my determination to explore Malaysia.

I daydream throughout the bus trip from Singapore to Mersing, where I catch the ferry to Pulau Tioman. We are decanted – a ragged band of backpackers – on the outskirts of the town, prey to the scam set up by the nearby travel agent, who insists that we book both ferry and hotels through him. I have phoned ahead, but can see those beside me lured into overcharges and feel powerless to help them. Or maybe this is just smug parental experience, and I am right to leave them to find out for themselves.

Our minibus arrives at the terminal just as the boat leaves; we have half an hour to wait. I bypass the convenient café and cross to a corner strewn with tables and plants. Flies buzz. Leaves rustle in the breeze, natural fans. Nothing hurries. Mersing is beginning to soothe me.

The only food left in the tiny Perspex cabinet is an 'apple pie' – with pastry, yes, then a dark layer that I believe to be apple, and yellow crusted layer that could be anything. But it is manna to me: sweet, slippery, sinful. I sit with my treasure and open my book; but not for long.

The café-owner, a round, loud-voiced man who

immediately gives his name as Omar, plonks beside me. We begin with the usual travelling questions: where am I from, where in England?

'I have spent time in Hereford,' he tells me. 'In England, one thing I don't understand, people will not talk to you.' It is an extraordinary prelude to a conversation. He takes no notice of my reticence. 'If I was in a café, like this, always alone; no one would sit with me. So I asked someone, in a shop – I was buying sunglasses – why do you not talk with people? She said that it's because you live inside, while we – all the time outside.' I cannot begin to explain that his brown skin may be part of the story. 'But I like your English. They were good for Malaysia; before Independence, before they leave, they spend ten years educating Malay lawyers and civil servants in the UK, so the country was ready. And now, we are a successful country. You know why?'

This sounds dangerously like politics; I contribute nodding. I can't work out if he is simply practising his English, proselytizing his gospel, or even chatting me up (goodness, I can't recall the last time that happened!). I decide it doesn't matter; he is expansive, and entertaining. Besides, I'll be gone in half an hour.

'A large middle class,' Omar persists. 'Every successful economy has a large middle class. With a large middle class you can build business. But things in your country – not so good since Margaret Thatcher. Margaret Thatcher destroyed truly representative democracy in the UK; but now maybe the House of Commons will force a vote of no confidence on Tony Blair and thus force his resignation and everything is better[1]. Tony Blair, he copy George Bush, and he – how can he believe he can create a democracy in Iraq? You cannot create a democracy, it must grow. Hugo Chavez – now he stands up to Bush, and he has done much for his poor people ...' I cling to

---

[1] Our conversation took place just after Labour had lost a by-election.

my 'no politics' decision; but need not worry. He is performing for an audience – and I am amply entertained.

Then suddenly he pauses, looks at me as if expecting a reply. I want to tell him that I was listening, honestly. In desperation I ask about the notice swinging above his head: 'Expedition Robinson'.

'I do the consultant,' Omar explains, 'for the TV. You know *Survivor*? It is filmed here, on the islands. That is why I go to England; and they come from Denmark and Norway, from all over. I arrange it all here – the hotels, the islands. You think they are just left there – but it is organised. So much crew. Nothing must go wrong. Soon they will be here again; it will be very busy.'

I am still grinning as I clamber on board the ferry. I have no idea if there is any truth in the *Survivor* story, nor where he gleans his political opinions. He reminds me of a man I knew as a child; he lived opposite us and spent most of his time tending his front garden as a pretext for engaging any passing pedestrian in the issues of the day. Omar has reminded me why I am here – to meet people like him!

And I have misjudged him. We meet again, a week later, on my return from Pulau Tioman. This time I am settled with a sandwich (no apple pie on offer) when he drags a chair beside me and waves behind the counter for coffee.

'I have no time. The programme. It is all beginning. So busy. Norway has day one tomorrow, Holland the day after, and then Belgium.' He reaches for his phone, apologises and explains: 'I must co-ordinate everything. They want a plane crash; I try to find someone to build it. A fire, tangled metal – all must be arranged. They cannot decide if they need bodies – I think they will need bodies. It must all be in the right place.' A helicopter roars overhead, defeating conversation for a couple of minutes, and sinks into the field behind us. There is the stink of engine and diesel.

'Refuelling. All day they go backwards and forwards. So much to do.' He is sitting on the edge of his seat, eyes flicking from the helicopter to the skies to his phone. 'Some people, they do not like all this. Too noisy, and all these foreigners. But it is good for Malaysia. We are on TV all over the world; everyone will see us, want to come here. Maybe your Tony Blair will come.'

I still can't decide if I want to talk about Tony Blair. In spite of BBC World and the World Service on my little radio, I feel very out of touch with politics at home. But I do want to carry on listening to Omar.

He pre-empts me; scrapes his chair back. 'Sorry, no time.' He bounds off towards the helicopter; his coffee grows cold.

47.

I spend the week between my two conversations with Omar on Pulau Tioman, an island off the south-east coast of Malaysia. *South Pacific* was filmed on Pulau Tioman. Sailors cavorted in its seas; Mary Martin washed that man right out of her hair with its soft tropical waters. There can be no better place for a dame to recover from a disorientating week at home.

Tropical islands attract more than their fair share of clichés. They are, we are told, idyllic, tranquil, carefree, disconnected from the hurly-burly, restorative, luxurious, bathed in glorious sunshine, with white-sand beaches and a backdrop of palm trees that rustle in the breeze. All of which makes Tioman impossible to describe without sounding like a holiday brochure.

I am staying in Air Batang, known (for reasons I never discover) as ABC. It consists of a pathway, just wide enough for a motorbike, connecting the motley collection of restaurants and lodges scattered along the foreshore. There are barely thirty metres of flat land in places before the ground rises steeply, covered in dense jungle, mysteriously green, and home, amongst other things, to marauding monkeys. My wooden hut, positioned a short way up the slope and raised on stilts as protection from tropical rainfall rushing down the hillsides, smells of trees; wet patches on the bathroom floor show leaky evidence of recent rain. Steam rises from foliage pressed against my window.

Hibiscus, in vulgar pink, is scattered alongside the pathway between me and the sea. The beach here is slightly stony, the waves shushing gently as they drift beneath the raised restaurant – a shack built above the water. A few hundred yards to the south and there is clean white sand, soft as icing sugar. To the north: a rocky headland, and footpath to another village. And, in between, the sea – sweetly clear, as sea is meant to be. The first time I swim I am confused by the dark shape that accompanies me, until I realise it is my shadow – unimpeded on the sandy seabed. Bright corals and tiny fish lure snorkellers into deeper waters. I am assured that a turtle is lurking beneath the rocks on the headlands, but it never comes out to play while I am swimming.

I loiter on the rusty chairs on my balcony, gazing at the giant trees around me – heavy with coconuts, bananas, jackfruit, papayas; invisible birds twitter. A distant baby cries. Rubbish is being burnt in a corner but the smoke wafts the other way and I cannot smell it. A black and white butterfly the size of the palm of my hand flutters by, followed by a yellow one, the size of the baby's. A monitor lizard ambles along the path, swishing its body with the arrogance of a model on a catwalk, tongue flicking at insects. Mynah birds scavenge. I am never far from a stubby-tailed ginger cat: the males have particularly proud testicles. A man carries a basket of washing out of a hut and drapes white sheets and orange blankets between trees.

Yes, this is idyllic. I could be writing the travelogue for a holiday paradise. So very different from the holidays of my childhood, in Torquay, North Wales, Ilfracombe. Huddled in raincoats, pretending we quite enjoyed being cold and wet. Sandcastles hold together quite well in the rain. Even my daughters – we took them to Pembrokeshire and Cornwall, and – once – to Venice – know all about wet holidays. I hope they will come here one day.

I have come here for the quiet. I need to give my head time to catch up with the demands I've made on my body. So I'm not quite sure how I manage to fall into so many conversations.

Hannah and Richard call across to me as I arrive at Nazri's bar one evening. She has wild, dark hair and wears a floral sundress, fluttering her cleavage at Richard who takes no notice. She leans across to me; already there is beer on her breath, and the sun has not long set. She lights one cigarette from the stub of another as I sit down. Richard, a slight, sandy Dutchman, reaches out to shake my hand, then relapses into silence.

'We are friends,' Hannah tells me repeatedly. I have no idea why she thinks their arrangements would trouble me. 'We travel, that is what we do. We have retired, you see.' Pause to sip her beer. 'We have a kitty, share the costs. Sometimes we take turns to pay. Just friends. That's how it works for us. We love it here; we'll be here for ten days, and then probably to Bali.' Drag on the cigarette. 'It is easy, though my luggage is heavy. I must have at least eight books. I cannot be without books.' Slurp the beer.

What does she want me to contribute to this conversation? It is, oddly, reminiscent, of women who came to me for counselling, trawling through sundry aspects of their lives while I try to work out what they are really trying to tell me. But I didn't come here to work.

'I find books in hostels and hotels, have read all sorts of things I wouldn't have looked at before,' I say; maybe we can talk about books.

'Oh no. I must choose my own books. You see, we have a flat in Bangkok,' puff, slurp. 'My parents come from Wales for two months every year, and join us there.' Her sentences don't quite link together; my mind hurries to keep up with her. She waves her glass, but the booze level, fortunately, is too low for it to spill. 'My mother, every year they come, from Wales. She is seventy now, had to buy a new rucksack last time she came. Not so easy in Wales.' A long cigarette pause. I concentrate on my beer.

'We have no home,' she persists. 'The flat is where we stay when my parents come from Wales to see us. I worry about them in the streets,' slurp; 'Bangkok is a bit different from Wales.' Puff. 'But we don't need to stay anywhere; we are both retired, and can just be where we want to be.' Why is she apparently proud of her homelessness when she is so repetitive about her roots? I have no intention of asking her, for fear she might tell me the answer.

She lights another cigarette; Richard has rustled a bird book from his bag and is holding it up to catch enough light to read. I take advantage of her puffing to contribute my own history.

'I can't imagine not having a home to return to,' I say. 'Maybe it's only possible for me to travel like this because I have got a home – and friends and family – waiting for me.' It sounds odd to hear the words out loud – as if I didn't know that was what I thought until I heard myself articulate them.

I'm the only one who seems to notice that I spoke; Hannah is off again. 'I never wanted children. I was a teacher; children are fine in the classroom but I never wanted them at home. I did some TEFL for a while. I'm 41 now, don't miss them.' Slurp – she waves an empty glass at Richard and he lurches across to the bar to refill it.

As soon as his back is turned she leans across to me. 'Your husband? How did he die, you don't mind me asking?' She has astonished me; unable to think quickly I provide a potted account of cancer and surgery. But I stick to the briefest details. She does not need to know about hours spent in a visitors' room in the hospital, a room that smelled of rich tea biscuits and coffee. Nor standing beside his bed, trying to explain to the nothingness of him that the tubes and wires will have to stay a bit longer, while the transplant teams lurch into action. I confide the briefest of details, but still Hannah's eyes prick with tears; she turns away in her distress and I wonder if I should apologise for upsetting her. What bubble have I pierced? Surely she should be making sympathetic noises to me? She stretches for her drink before Richard has put it on the table.

'I wish they'd turn the noise down.' It is the first time I've heard his thick accent. Phew; this is enough to direct Hannah onto a different path.

'There is nothing else for them to do here.' (I think she means the Malays.) Slurp. 'But most of them are on dope anyway, and the bartender here – he's alcoholic; at least I think he is.' Time for another cigarette. 'And they're so fat – going everywhere on motorbikes, don't even walk anywhere.' Slurp. 'But I suppose there's nothing much else for them to do, bits of tourism and maybe a bit of fishing.'

There is no peace in her. But she has made me think. Oh, I know it looks idyllic, meandering from Pulau Tioman to Bali with the occasional sojourn in Bangkok. No ties, no repose. Nothing – no front door that swells in the rain and needs a judicious shove to open it; no fields or forests or moorland with her footprints lingering in the mud; no crowded bookshelves with the pristine copy of Seamus Heaney's poetry unopened at the back. No one to love. No, I do not envy them.

All this musing! On top of my grand-maternal longings! That is how I explain being ill. I've careered around the world; my emotions as well as my body have taken flight. What do I expect?

I had not expected the assault on my throat, sinuses, ears and teeth that takes over my head. This is not a book about being ill, any more than it's a book about babies. But this illness eats into my days, wakes me at night. I treat it with rest (to begin with), and finally break open the packet of antibiotics I have with me. For a day or so I believe they are working. And then the throbbing sets off again; I can hear little but ringing; my mouth tastes of metal; my throat is ravaged by knives. My thinking fractures. The second set of antibiotics take days to bring the pain under control.

I don't want to be ill. More than that – I don't want to be ill here. I refuse to spend glorious afternoons in bed when the sand beckons. I admit – with some reluctance – that snorkelling is probably a bad idea. I submit to beer-restrictions while taking antibiotics. I can't quite gather myself to walk across the island through the jungle, in spite of the lure of a close encounter with a monkey. But that is as far as I am prepared to go. I continue to potter around the village, to drift in and out of the sea, to read and write as usual. Given the uncertain electricity supply going to bed early is expected.

Foolish? Almost certainly. But illness – not illness that lingers like this – was never part of the plan and I find it impossible to incorporate it into my thinking now. For days, weeks even, my diary is testament to a general weariness. It seems I am willing to commit that realisation to paper, but refuse to allow it access to the common sense corner of my mind which might urge me to rest. Even here, in this book, it is relegated to the smallest section. But it loiters in the scenery for weeks to come, and provides the backdrop for the drama which will finally bring me home.

48.

Why am I leaving Pulau Tioman? I flirt with the idea of staying here for another five months, of blogging a fictional trip while I lounge about on distant sands, a fantasy which is oddly reminiscent of my thoughts of spending a year in a hotel at Heathrow, but in far kinder surroundings. I suppose my decision to leave as planned can only be put down to bloody-mindedness, when common sense would suggest that arrangements to head into the jungle could be changed with a phone call and my body was screaming for rest.

But had I stayed, I might have missed meeting Rocky.

She runs a hostel in Mersing, nestling behind a yellow door and up a flight of shabby stairs. Ahead I find a narrow room, sofas along each side, a desk, a television buzzing with an American cop show, and a fish tank – its occupant so huge I doubt if it can turn round. I flop on a sofa and wait.

It takes ten minutes for Rocky to appear. Everything about her is round, even the dimples on her knees. She takes one look at me, disappears without a word, returning with a pot of tea, milk jug, sugar in a bowl and cups and saucers decorated with pink roses.

'I can always tell,' she announces. 'I always know when someone needs a cup of tea.' She clucks around me; within minutes we are chatting as women, about food, and Mersing, and the need for tea. Her son, equally round, clumps in. He disappears; we have no way of knowing what he is doing, but before long he slinks wordlessly down the stairs.

'He is fifteen,' she says, no other explanation needed. We talk about our offspring; I show her a photograph of the baby and she drools; I preen. We both know the script.

Later that evening Rocky's husband, Anwar, arrives home from taking tourists on a jungle trek. He is slight, wiry, with a pointy beard which once, I was told, reached down to his waist. He wanders from room to room, fidgets in chairs; he seems uncomfortable with the restrictions of being indoors. For a small man he takes up a lot of space. I am urged to join them for supper, find myself with a pizza and lime juice on my knee, the television in full cry.

Plates hidden in the kitchen, and Rocky gathers herself for a trip to the supermarket; Anwar leads another trek into the jungle tomorrow and needs provisions.

'Can I join you?' It seems an odd thing to ask, to join in a supermarket shop. As if grocery shopping is a novelty. But I know Rocky will lead me into places I wouldn't have considered on my own. She is greeted by friends and shopkeepers at every turn. The supermarket aisles are too narrow for both of us, crammed with great sacks of rice, packets of spices, bottles of sauces and oils, the dusty smell of grains. We each lug two bags of shopping, plastic bags cutting into our fingers, but have been unable to find corned beef and cigarettes for Anwar. We head off on a cigarette-hunt – successful only after searching in three different shops. Rocky chats all the time, and I learn more about the impact of the scam that had abandoned me on the edge of Mersing when I arrived here a week ago.

'We complain to the police, to the tourist office. But they do nothing. The bus company, the ferries, the hotels – they are all in it. But people like me, I will not join in – and now no one walks past my hostel, people do not call in here. We lose business, but can do nothing. And not just me; travel agents in town, by the ferry, they lose too. But we can do nothing; we lose money and no one will help us.'

On our return she shows me letters she has written, but there have been no replies. She leaves me with feelings of outrage, and helplessness, and I wish I could do something to help. Old rescuing feelings stir; they sent me into social work so long ago. I post warnings on the *Lonely Planet* website; it absolves my conscience just a little; I doubt if anything changes.

Anwar is prowling when I come down for breakfast; eventually he grabs a ragged backpack and a couple of plastic bags, looking more comfortable with his luggage on his back. And then, without preamble, he is gone. The house is unnaturally quiet; Oprah Winfrey entertains Rocky and me as we eat breakfast. Her son slumps through the room.

'I had four boys,' she tells me, 'but one died two weeks ago.' I am horrified, but the story is more complex than this stark announcement. She reaches for a photograph.

'He was with me for three years, but he was alcoholic. He

was a lovely boy, see he is smiling here; he could not do enough for me.' She brings out a picture of a thin lad, bambi-legged, spread-eagled where I am sitting now.

'He couldn't stop the drinking; I know he tried. He went away; I think he didn't want to upset me by dying here. And he didn't go to his mother – he didn't want to upset her either. He was in KL, on his own. So I couldn't say goodbye to him.' I nod, wait for tears, but they don't come.

'I do the best for him; they say prayers for him at the mosque. I have no time to go, to say the prayers, so I make food for them to give to the poor and then they pray for him. I know they pray for him. He will be at peace now; he was a lovely boy but he was troubled, always troubled.' Her distress is curtailed when another couple of guests appear looking for breakfast; time for me to slip away.

It is a harrowing tale to piece together. Was he fostered? A guest, as I am, who lingered for weeks, months, longer? I don't understand the nuances of the script. But Rocky's grief is tangible; it hangs in the room like fog.

It is time to leave; I have to catch a bus to KL. Rocky is tired this morning; she had no sleep, she explains, as she is worrying – worrying about the bills. Anwar does not understand; he is not a businessman. She frets alone.

'I must pay you, Rocky – how much do I owe you?' She finds a tatty piece of paper, adds up the room, my pizza, and struggles to reach a total of thirty-five ringgits (about five pounds).

'Rocky, this is why you have no money. What about all the cups of tea, the lime juice?'

'I do not charge for them.' Rocky is horrified. 'They are just drinks.' But I seize her piece of paper, add what I can, include a tip, and give her fifty ringgits; she hugs me and I promise to return. It feels as if I have known her for years.

49.

The bus trundles towards Taman Nagara, a National Park in the Malaysian jungle. It is a long slow chug up green hillsides, the road winding this way and that, mostly through rainforest (I manage to spot one monkey and one large bird of prey), the occasional palm tree or rubber plantations, a village or two, some crisp modern bungalows with impressive vehicles in small car-ports, a few crumbly, wooden traditional houses with no evidence of habitation, and two roadside eateries. Whatever am I doing here? I mean, my *Lonely Planet* warns me about leeches!

I've grown a little more sanguine about insects during the last few months. At home I don't take kindly to any insect larger than an ant. Now I can shrug off cockroaches, and no longer feel it necessary to swat every mosquito. But leeches – even the word brings the sting of bile to my throat. They will suck my blood, like vampires.

Yet here I am. Why? Because I'll regret it if I don't.

The final part of the journey involves a two-hour roar up the Tembeling River in a dugout canoe, armed with an outboard motor. There are no seats, just plastic cushions to soften the journey. The river, stained with a mud-brown legacy of logging upstream, winds through dense jungle. At first glance all is dressed in a patchwork of green, but closer inspection reveals glorious orange bracts, a tree resembling lilac with wonderful purple blossoms. We pass occasional sandbanks, grassy clearings grazed short by water buffalo. Everything smells drippingly wet. My travelling companions – all at least half my age – fall asleep; I prop myself, uncomfortably, and relish every moment.

I have a 'hotel' booked in Kuala Tahan, a scruffy village on the opposite side of the river from a choreographed resort. The first hazard: a climb up a steep and muddy slope with my rucksack on; I stare at my feet, think about one step at a time, have to resort to sinking fingers into the mud to scramble up the last steps. As I reach the top I wipe the hair from my eyes, mirroring the mud-streaks down my skirt with an elegant swipe. I was never good at glamour.

My wooden hut is at the top of the small cliff. Inside I have a bed, *sellotape* failing to secure all the holes in the mosquito net, a small cupboard, and a broom and dustpan anticipating an invasion of sand and mud. The shutters don't quite fit the windows; the nylon curtains an alarming floral pink. Behind is a bathroom – a dark, tin add-on, somehow smelling of cabbage. The towels are so thin even my war-weary mother would have thrown them away. But the river sweeps persistently by; small chickens find something nourishing in the grass; a cat plays tigers in the scrub beyond. A determined bird repeats his little song; a hornbill swoops across the river and disappears into thick green trees. A boat groans by. The air smells of damp and mud, the humidity so high that even breathing makes me sweat.

Muddy huts hide in corners all along the bank, some more sturdy and glamorous than others. Behind them are traditional homes for the Malays, built on stilts – protection from monsoon rains flooding the hillsides, I presume.

Between my hut and theirs is a row of sheds, which may be toilets; one green door is firmly closed with a notice: SNAKE. DO NOT ENTER. I wouldn't dream of it, though could be tempted to peek under the door if the gap were a little wider.

I slither down the bank to the floating restaurant, just as the insects set up their early evening chorus. But I have barely opened my diary when Russell and Tamsin, two of my young companions in the dugout, slide into the seats beside me. He is a sturdy man, his curly hair flecked with red, eyes a surprising blue. Tamsin is more delicate, with unblemished skin and hazel eyes that glance, repeatedly, at him. There are the usual introductions. Russell, I learn, was brought up just ten miles from my home. We talk about Wiltshire, and the Newbury bypass, the crisp air of the Downs and sogginess of fields in winter. It nourishes me, this link with home. I feel, briefly, understood.

But Tamsin must have her say. She tells me that they are on honeymoon; a journey that will take six months and end in a house they are building in Kenya, grounded ecologically; eventually it will be a retreat for tourists. I am shown a photograph of an elegant terrace with a view sweeping across African sand. Of course, she insists, they have a flat in London as well. I flounder; I have nothing to say to her. I want to talk about Wiltshire.

We must meet tomorrow, they insist. Arrangements are easily made. The village being too small for choices, 'at breakfast' is sufficiently accurate to be sure we'll meet at some stage. They help me find a route back to my hut that does not involve clambering through mud, then slink off into the darkness.

I have grown accustomed to passing conversations, with all their surprises. But I don't understand the persistence of Russell and Tamsin. Do they think I need looking after? Do they believe I am lonely? Need some form of supervision, a chaperone, that I'll land myself in some metaphorical doo-doo without them? Are they simply kind, lonely in spite of each other, entertained by my tales? Or maybe I remind them of a mother. I am hardly in a position to examine anyone's motives too closely.

Russell and Tamsin are, it turns out, ideal companions for the jungle. He is a quietly attentive man. She is a biologist, with a specific interest in tropical insects. We pause to inspect an army of termites busily chewing through wood, large red-bottomed ants, a leech (yuk) waving its tiny head out of the ground, an orange centipede in a hurry. Tamsin is in heaven: each new discovery is greeted with the rapture of a pirate with his treasure. She wonders why this ant – unlike most ants – is found alone; she demonstrates the urgency with which the leech makes for her blood-warmth, disappointing it by removing her hand just in time. She inspects every tendril on the centipede before removing it from the pathway and warning me of its poisonous potential. I am almost interested.

It is their idea to take a canoe trip. A ferry takes us across to a small boatyard and we settle into canoes – two by two. On with the safety helmets, blue life jackets, and plastic shoes in case we fall in. To my initial alarm I have the guide to myself – a slight, muscular man with a name I cannot pronounce and so we agree on Zam.

I seize the oar with enthusiasm but without skill, wave it around in the water, knowing that he is doing all the work. Within ten minutes we leave Russell and Tamsin struggling with the first rapids – while they paddle persistently and without reward Zam leaps into the river and shoves us through the rushing waters. Over and over, whenever the river shallows, I turn to see him up to his thighs in water, pushing. Only once is it necessary for me to clamber out with him; he gives me an oar to steady my footing on the slippery stones on the riverbed, stretches an arm for me to grab if I should feel unsteady. Do I look that old? I know the answer to that.

'Your friends?' Zam asks. I shrug; the river is too wonderful for me to worry about them. He asks where I am from, do I like Malaysia, completing every sentence with a nervous giggle. He rises to my questions about the river, the name of this bird, the fruit of that tree, the lives of those living in the forest, puffing his chest with pride in his answers.

'The forest, is the oldest in the world. One hundred and fifty thousand years old. The oldest living trees are here.' He names blossoms and shrubs, but few survive in my memory long enough to reach the diary. He reaches up to pull a woody fruit that looks like small acorns, insists that I eat it. It is, he tells me, called a jumbu-i, but given his giggling he might be teaching me the Malay for knickers. We see a kingfisher decorated with all the colours of a child's painting, a hornbill, some tiny navy birds that dart across the water, diving for insects. He finds nests – hanging constructions of reeds and grasses, huge assortments of twigs in the treetops.

Time takes over; he insists that we must turn round. I cannot argue, and plunge my oar regretfully back into the water as we head for home.

'No, paddle.' He is adamant. 'You relax.'

And so we drift back down the river, listening only to the forest preparing itself for the night. It sings with insects: crickets and cicadas, with added rattles and scratches; and then the occasional twitter and whoop and finally the full repertoire of Malaysian birdsong. I turn my head this way and that, but all choristers are safely hidden in the foliage. The air is ripe with the smells of trees, and river, and – on one corner only – the stink of dead animal. Crows scream. Vultures circle. I wish I could float here forever.

We are late back; he does not charge me for the extra time and I tip him handsomely; we are both happy.

But Russell and Tamsin are still on the river. They have been examining insect mounds and animal tracks along the bank and are unaware of the concern mounting in the boatyard as the night draws swiftly in. Zam goes to look for them; still they do not hurry; Tamsin thinks it is sweet that anyone should worry about them. I wonder when she last spoke to her mother.

50.

We gather later, over supper, joined by Paul and Cathy – younger even than Russell and Tamsin. They are unsettled, with no plans and no money. Paul talks vaguely of maybe working long enough to keep travelling but Cathy toys with thoughts of training to be a teacher, or maybe a nurse. When I reach for my diary later I find them difficult to describe; it is as if they are not yet fully formed. Probably a bit like I would have been, if I'd ever made it this far in my early twenties.

Paul and Cathy are preoccupied with trying to find some dope; they have run out, and need more. They talk as if I'm not there; I can't believe they would talk like this in front of their parents, and can only assume the familiar role of an invisible. It makes me smile now, after so long being noticed.

'We must be able to get some around here, if we only knew where to look.' Paul is insistent. 'Can't believe there just isn't any.' His fingers tap rhythmically on the table; his knees fidget.

'It was everywhere in Thailand,' Russell agrees. 'And with no problems – it was great stuff. Everyone just lying about, smoking a bit of this, a bit of that.'

The four of them compare prices, strength, availability on the various islands they have visited. There is general agreement that drug-use in Thailand is overlooked by the police, that only the foolish get caught and imprisoned, that only the unwary would fail to spot adulterated weed or underweight spliffs.

For a moment Russell seems to remember that I'm there; he asks if I have ever used drugs and I remind him that I was young in the Sixties. But no one stops to listen to my comments; they are too absorbed in their my-drugs-are-stronger-than-your-drugs conversation to take any notice of me.

'We got rid of ours before crossing the border,' Tamsin announces, with a sanctimonious look on her face. I have no idea who she is trying to impress. 'There are too many tales of people in prison in Malaysia, we couldn't risk getting caught with it, spending years behind bars. It's just not worth it.'

'No way – we got some through, no problem.' The prospect of imprisonment seems a new idea to Paul. 'Just hide it in your pants, like we do, and get straight through. No idea what the fuss is about.'

They launch into a competition as to who had taken the biggest stash through which borders. But it doesn't take Paul long to return to his need to buy more; maybe he is hoping that Russell is fibbing and has, in fact, secreted some in his underwear.

'We might even have to go back to Thailand,' he says, 'given how difficult it seems to be finding any here. Can't go on for long like this.'

'We miss it,' Russell agrees. 'But we knew we'd have to manage while we were here. It's fine, if you know that's what you have to do. But we smoke every evening at home. Can't see what all the fuss is about, just a bit of weed. Nice and calm at the end of the day. In Kenya, we keep it from the natives. Don't want them getting into any bother, so it's best if they don't know. (I think he means their staff.) We have to be a bit careful there, can't risk hassles from the police. But haven't had any problems so far.'

'It just helps to relax, after the day,' Tamsin contributes. Her fingers flick on the table, as if holding a cigarette. The discussion has made them all a little jumpy.

I keep my own counsel – not that they would be interested in the opinion of a woman in her mid-fifties even if I were to give it. I am amused that they had the discussion in front of me; it takes me outside the role of surrogate parent or teacher – to be what, exactly? My relation with them has no parallel in a social set-up.

Yet their disregard for my existence – in such contrast to our walk in the jungle when Tamsin was so keen to talk of insects and Russell of the green grass of home – lodged me in the familiar position of old fogey, unimportant, unseen. What they couldn't possibly know was how entertaining they were.

Even so, I have to swallow pompous disapproval of their eagerness to throw anything down their throats. I can't envy Paul and Cathy's demands for pleasure without thought for tomorrow.

Then I cringe at my stuffiness, and wish I had the wherewithal to make a cup of tea.

51.

Back down the river, savouring my final chug along its muddy waters, the last breaths of steaming forest. Two buses. My rucksack has lost another strand of tinsel. The last two wisps look lost, forgotten. But I cannot take them off, hide them in the depths of my rucksack in the hope they will survive that way. I am heading for the Cameron Highlands.

The guidebooks have told me to expected green, tea-plantation beauty. But, as the bus staggers up the steep hillside, I am appalled by the fractured scenery. The air is cooler as we climb, making agriculture easier; but once-forested hillsides are now steeply terraced, leaving red-brown topsoil streaming down and gathering in muddy rivers in the valleys. Denuded, many fields are no longer fertile. As we climb higher I spot the new solution: poly-tunnels. Of course Malaysia must feed herself. I peer inside as we drive past but spot only chrysanthemums, white, yellow and pink (is this where Tesco's source their bunches for £2.99?). I wallow, briefly, in environmental pedantry; then work at reminding myself I know too little of the area to be making such instant judgements.

My punishment – a tropical storm. Our driver condescends to slow slightly; how he can see, even with his wipers on full speed, I have no idea. The noise of the engine is drowned by hail pounding on the roof of the bus; small rivers tumble down each side of the road. We pass a market shrouded in blue tarpaulins. I have a fantasy of trying to find my hotel in Tanah Rata armed only with my soggy *Lonely Planet*, punishment for my environmental arrogance. I need not have worried; in twenty minutes it is over.

I need a quiet day, after all that jungle excitement. Tanah Rata is crammed with souvenir shops and tiny supermarkets, little cafés that specialise in fragrant Malaysian tea. Squeezed in a corner, I find a reflexology massage centre. At home I would check out qualifications, google professional bodies. Here – I just walk in, because I feel like it.

My feet and lower legs are smothered in cold cream, the smell an instant reminder of school plays. This is followed by a methodical, purposeful, millimetre-by-millimetre investigation of every corner of my feet. Every ache and pain I've ever known is quietly soothed away. My masseur – a tiny man with kind eyes and magic fingers – locates an old shoulder injury, then probes a corner near my ankle.

'You have a headache,' he says.

'No, no headache.'

'Yes, there is headache; there is a problem here, in your head.' He taps his skull – he is not referring to my recent throat or ear problems. I shrug; it means nothing to me; but he repeats his insistence that my head is suffering. The moment passes, remembered only in the pages of my diary. Only one month later his warnings will come back to haunt me. I will recall his penetrating eyes and soothing fingers and wish I'd listened. For now – I lie back, think of anything but England, and feel truly restored. I have no idea if it has done me any good, but I savour it anyway.

The massage has given me an illusion of vigour. I grab a backpack and join a jungle trek; it will last just three-to-four hours. I can manage that. We gather at the front of the hotel; our guide, a wiry Indian named Kali, is the only person older than me; everyone else must be under thirty. But they are patient with my puffing up the sticky hills, my gasping for breath from heat and altitude, and my need for a helping hand up rocky or slippery bits. The paths are, almost without exception, muddy. I have no doubt that Tamsin would be in insect heaven. (One woman flicks a leech off her leg without screeching; I am most impressed.)

Kali, of course, bounds without puffing. His father introduced him to the jungle and now he has retired from his work in a bank he can spend all his time trekking its paths. He knows every inch.

He crunches leaves. 'Here, you smell this.' He passes squished juices from palm to palm, scented with spinach, fennel, citronella, *Germolene*! (Maybe the previous occupant of my cell in KL came from here.) He drops tiny wild strawberries into our mouths, makes bracelets from rattan, umbrellas from banana leaves.

'This leaf,' he points into dense foliage, 'this you can eat, but only if you are in the jungle for a long time. Only then is it good.' He crushes wild betel palm onto our hands, shows how it reddens skin; points to huge droops of carnivorous plants ready for curious insects. He finds a millipede curled like a tiny nut; another, twenty-five centimetres long, is allowed to unfurl and creep along his arm. It is a different enthusiasm from Tamsin's; her's has grown from years of academic study, while he has absorbed the mores of the jungle from infancy. They have a different authenticity. Some of the young people are merely polite to him, but I am hypnotised – by his knowledge, his passion for the rainforest.

We clamber muddy slopes behind him, slither down again, push through clinging undergrowth, leap across rushing streams. (Well, the others leap. I perch on the bank and hands grab me as I throw myself in the right direction.)

It is a surprise when we emerge by a roadside and a small café with plates of delicacies for lunch: rice parcels in banana leaves, a coconut sesame ball, fried bananas, something that looks like uncooked dough, spring rolls, phallic doughnuts. We are invited to try everything; it is a symphony of tastes and within half an hour the plates are empty. Kali gathers us.

Only then do I realise that the walk will last all day. No problem; I feel fine.

A minibus takes us to another tea plantation; we obediently watch a promotional video, trail around the factory, and then a climb to a viewpoint for a vista of the plantation, familiar to me from Kerala, but still beautiful. There are no poly-tunnels here, just the patchwork of greens sweeping across gentle hillsides. If they grew tea in Wiltshire it would look like this. Kali wants to hurry us down; we defy him and linger.

What fools! He knows the skies, laughs as we struggle into waterproofs before giving up and running back to the plantation café, water dripping from hair and noses, wet through to our knickers. I am, of course, last; my middle-aged waddle no match for the strides of my companions. But they are kind, ply me with sweet tea while our clothes drip and rain hammers outside.

The rain eases only half an hour later. Steam rises from the sodden earth. There is an alluring smell of wet leaves and clean pathways. We wander back into the plantation, dropping down between the rows of tea trees to a road where a passing pick-up truck piles us all in somehow, squeezing his vegetables into a corner away from our mud and sweatiness. He leaves us at a farm where we join the last paths home.

Here, unpredictably, I struggle.

As the path turns steeply uphill, my body decides it has had enough. I reel slightly as if I have lost the switch marked 'walking'. I don't recognise my body; it has never done this to me before and I don't know how to nurture it. Suddenly lying down in the mud and going to sleep seems inviting. That, I know, clinging to common sense, is not an option. I force step after step, drop further and further behind. Muscles fight back; my head spins; my ears rush; Kali reaches for my hand and helps me to sit, forces biscuits and glucose sweets on me.

'It is all flat now,' he lies.

Every step becomes a challenge; the youngsters give up waiting for me. I don't blame them. Only Kali and a sturdy Australian couple stay with me. Kali plies me with pineapple juice, makes no comment on my wandering footsteps. I have no idea what is happening to me, only that I want this to end.

There is no recourse to taxis in the jungle. I have to walk, and walk. The Australian couple prattle about nothing, do their best to keep my mind from wandering. I have an urgent toilet need, stagger to the bus station, evacuate explosively and copiously, notice how my body is shutting down every process it doesn't need in current circumstances (I find this interesting, as if it has nothing to do with me). Now I am more comfortable, totter the final half-mile, manage a small plate of noodles and flop gratefully into bed.

I am less stiff than I deserve. Tree frogs click outside while I settle to sleep.

52.

All I need is a rest. This is just a blip, like the sore throat on Tioman, the warnings of my masseur. One day in bed, and then I am on my way. But my body is trying to tell me something and I will not listen. At my age I should know better.

Penang is my last stop in Malaysia. And I love it. It's a multicultural soup of a city, with Chinese, Malays, Thais jostling with Australians and New Zealanders who are beginning to develop businesses here.

Just left of my hotel is Lebuh Chulia, the main street of old Chinatown. It surprises me; I expect the bustle of Chinese streets such as those I saw in Singapore. But here there are only worn out, often shuttered, shops, with flaking paint and ill-fitting shutters. The drains whiff occasionally; there is a small market in a side street selling rice and grains – with a definite smell of rats. I had hoped to find presents here, to send home; instead I potter past fading shophouses, stand to admire stately arched window-frames, hints of once-flamboyant decorations on locked doors. There are a few cafés, a pawnbroker, a bottle shop, cut-price hostels.

The street takes a different shape in the evenings. Working girls hover in doorways; I notice one, thin legs poking from her tiny shorts, grabbing a punter by the genitals than waving five fingers at him (does she really only charge five ringgits?), repeating the exercise until she follows him into a dark corner.

Further down the road, a man with large shoulders and wearing a bright yellow dress chats to another, his beard incongruous above his long skirt.

On to explore Little India, busy with small shops and hawker stalls, gaudy clothes and pungent spices, bellowing music from CD and DVD shops. Beyond Little India to the coast, where I explore the Chinese clan jetties. These are central wooden platforms, about five metres wide, built from the shoreline and extending out to sea, with wooden homes tacked on each side. Water slops against stilts – originally made of wood, but many now replaced with concrete. Men chat on platforms; women lurk by open doorways in a lazy Sunday sort of way; children squat with their mothers. I peek through doorways, many decorated in auspicious red, into lino-covered hallways with a chair or two and small shrine.

As a middle-aged white woman, I disappear into this melting pot without comment. I meander through the streets, drift in and out of cafés, peer into temples, investigate the occasional monument. I agree to a tourist tour, but it lacks the excitement of discovering Penang for myself.

My days in Penang develop something of a routine. I always begin with breakfast in the same street café in Chinatown. It has, on the surface, little to recommend it. There are rarely any other guests; the tables are grubby and their legs wobble; chickens strut noisily (and stink), squabbling over small piles of rice; there are tales of rats as big as cats. Banks of plants in pots do their best to relieve the sense of dust and grey; there is a cage of birds that look to me like quail, but my waiter tells me that they are called 'local birds'.

Farouq, a yellow, cadaverous man with no teeth, round glasses and a protruding chin, seems to be the only person working here; and it is his curiosity that brings me back day after day. I begin with muesli, fruit, yogurt, toast and coffee; when I arrive on the second morning Farouq beams and produces an even more generous bowl of cereal, presses me to drink more mugs of coffee; as I leave he brushes my shoulder and mutters, 'Take care.' By the third morning I am welcomed with, 'There you are, my dear;' and the muesli bowl almost overflows. Extra toast – unasked for – is preceded only by the scratch of scraped burn from the kitchen.

On the fourth morning Farouq reaches to shake my hand. 'Do you do cooking? Washing?' I confirm that I do but he turns my hands over in disbelief. 'Your hands, so soft. You are a teacher?' I decide that is near enough, and agree that I am a teacher. But each time I bring out my camera he retreats, 'no photograph today, perhaps tomorrow.'

It is my last day. 'Today,' I try, 'please a photo today; I will not be here again.' He is wearing his most alarming shirt, arranges his fragile frame, refuses to reveal his gums by smiling, and consents to a rather grim photograph. It is not a fitting memento after all his kindness.

Farouq tries not to cling to my hand as we shake farewells. I cannot know what my visit means to him. I know only that his daily welcome sets me up for the day. He knows I'm here, notices my comings and goings. I hadn't realised I might be missing that.

In contrast, the late afternoon sees me in a bright café with alarming orange walls. The lure? Not the banks of computers, not the silent woman who seems to spend all day crouched over her laptop. No – cup after cup of the most delicious tea. A sop to my Englishness.

And one day I chat to Rob and Alice there. We agree to meet later for supper. They are weathered, with elegant clothes and easy, comfortable bodies. They must be, I decide, in their sixties.

'You should visit Lankawi,' they persist. 'It is the most beautiful island; we are building a house there. We came – it must be ten years ago when we came here first – always promised ourselves we'd retire here. It's hard, mind; we've had to get jungle cleared – bloody hard work that was. Did a few bits ourselves; had to get men in to do most of it. You should see it – it's like a proper Malay house, wooden; we've had it designed here; got local builders.'

I press them; 'How do you find it living here?'

'It's no problem – much like being at home really. You just get on with everyone.'

Just get on with everyone. Yes, I do get on with most people at home. But there is much more to 'home' than passing relationships – or maybe they have a different definition of 'getting on'. Apart from my week with the baby, I have been away for almost eight months. My diary begins to flirt with thoughts of home: not the bricks and mortar, but the idea of roots and foundations, and other mixed metaphors which seem to be the only way of describing my growing awareness of the depth of feeling for the place I come from. I wasn't born in Wiltshire; three of my daughters have moved away, though they visit frequently; but I belong there. Belong: it's a flimsy word for something so profound. I want to know how Rob and Alice negotiate a feeling of belonging, having moved to Lankawi.

But the owner of the restaurant interrupts my clumsy efforts to explain myself; he is a man they know well and they chatter about mutual friends. His wife invites me to explore the rest of the building; this is no time to wallow in philosophical discussions about the nature of home. I scuttle after her. This, like so many, is a converted shophouse. She leads me up steep stairs into four interlocking rooms in various states of disrepair, and all crammed with Malaysian memorabilia: old photographs, pots and pans, lamps, a doll's house made of bamboo, a 1950s telephone, a sewing machine, pipes (for smoking), baskets, a couple of old doors, cases, paintings, straw hats, crockery; fragments that would not have been out of place in my grandmother's house.

'One day I'll sort all this out. There were four families living here when we bought it – look at it.'

I look at it. 'You've a huge task – it's lovely, but there's so much that still needs sorting out.'

'Oh yes, and there are still people who want to pull it all down. At the moment we depend on the Press – if anyone wants to pull an old shophouse down the papers make a fuss; much quicker than going through any sort of appeal.'

'So you're dependent on individuals doing up each house?'

'Yes – and you should have seen it six years ago when we began the Penang Heritage Trust. It's so much better than it was. Come back in ten years, you won't recognise it.' I have an uncomfortable image of every building freshly-painted, manicured, pristine; I can't tell her that there is something about the seediness of the flaking corners of Penang that so appeals to me.

PART NINE

NOT THE END OF THE STORY

53.

I am off to Thailand. I have loved Malaysia, and vow to return. I might not be able to swing my rucksack about with the easy rhythms of the young, but I share their confidence now. And their conviction that nothing can go wrong. I feel foolishly immune to the possibility of problems that I cannot overcome.

The ferry crossing to the mainland is smooth enough, and the station is easy to find. I am unconcerned by a train delay. Three carriages trundle into the station eventually; we join a longer train later. There is no problem finding my berth – but another man, solid and insistent, claims the same place! We examine tickets, to discover that I have mistaken the day. I should have travelled yesterday; somewhere in my head the notion of arriving on June 2nd has translated into leaving on the 2nd.

There is no time to reflect that such mistakes are unlike me – made generally when I am overloaded or my thinking clouded, as it can be when I'm ill. It doesn't occur to me that there might be a lesson to think about here. The train is ready to depart; I wave at a steward, who takes a moment to understand the problem, then directs me towards a seat in a second carriage.

'Sit here; you pay 50 baht on the border; it is fine.' I know that there is an Asian aversion to losing face, that making mistakes is somehow shameful and must be censored. Is he protecting me from humiliation? Does he assume I'm a doddery old soul who makes mistakes like this all the time? Or is this the kindness of anyone wishing simply to help out? A ticket inspector trawls down the carriage; his English is better and he understands 'mistake'. He agrees I can pay nothing for the Malaysian section of the trip, but will have to shell out on the Thai side. Their reassurances are real and penetrating.

I settle into my seat. A family nearby seem to do nothing but eat; the children rustle endless packets of crisps and plastic boxes; they are initially appealing but less so once they are sugar-fuelled.

But my mind is absorbed with the challenge of crossing the border. Will there be a berth from here to Bangkok, or will I be squashed in a corner, upright, all night? I find the immigration office without a problem; a sour man, who refuses to raise his eyes from the paperwork in front of him, insists I must pay eight hundred and seventy baht.

'I was told it would be fifty baht?' I know I sound feeble. I have no weapons, neither the brazenness of youth nor the excuses of senility. He buries his face in the papers and repeats his insistence that I pay the full price. The border is isolated, and terrorists are reputed to be alive and well in this corner of Thailand. I pay his price; I am in no position to complain.

The guard emerges from his little cabin as I climb back into the train. 'Fifty baht?' he asks.

'No, much more.' I cannot tell him how much more. He frowns; I shrug. For the rest of the journey he tends to me as if I were the queen.

My berth is narrow but comfortable enough; the carriage smells of stale food and, of course, there is the rasp of snoring. In the morning I have a couple of hours staring out at acres of soggy, muddy paddy fields, palm and banana and mango plantations, and a few fleeting towns. Only one strand of tinsel survives the train journey.

My week at home, and the days to arrange and recover from it, has eaten time from my travelling. I can't see everything – and make it to St Petersburg for my flight home in October. What to miss out? Although I agonise for a day or two, the decision is obvious. Trips to Thailand are easy from the UK. There are daily flights from London. I shall spend just a few days in Bangkok, and promise to return one day.

54.

I clamber from the train and head for the nearest café; I need coffee. I am settled with my drink and diary when Anke taps me on the shoulder. She is freshly beautiful, fair-haired and blue-eyed, her skin blooming with youthful health. We soon establish that she is Dutch.

'You have a *Lonely Planet*? May I have a look? I think I might go to see the River Kwai Bridge.' I pull out my book, but have torn out all the pages I don't need (to make the book lighter) and so can't help her.

'I have been here for one day; I must decide what to do next.' She looks at me as if expecting an answer; I offer a second cup of coffee. I'm not sure why it seems rude to ask why she has come all this way on her own, and doesn't even have a guidebook. I've fielded comparable questions myself, many times, in the last few months.

'I have been here before, with my boyfriend, my ex-boyfriend,' she says. 'But now I come alone; I know it is easy here. I love it; you begin alone and the next minute – bam, you meet someone and find you are travelling together.'

'I think the River Kwai is south, towards Malaysia. There are parts of that region that are not safe for tourists. You will need to check.'

'Maybe I'll stay here for another day. I have no real plans. I didn't read books before I came; I just want to see how I feel, now I am here.' I will not worry about her; it would feel too much like mothering.

Nevertheless, we share a taxi, to save money; she checks into my hotel for one night. I have not finished showering when she taps on my door.

'You would like a beer?'

'I'd rather have a cup of tea.'

Bangkok buzzes around us as we sit in our corner café exchanging family histories.

'The thing is, my father died two years ago, two years ago this month. My stepmother, she is good to me; and I am, I suppose, close to her. It has been hard; I was so close to him.' She stops; I look away as I am sure she needs privacy for her weeping. Or does she? Something about her cries out for protection.

'But now, I need new things. My boyfriend – my ex-boyfriend – we are very good friends; he comes to see me from time to time, just turns up. But I think, now, it is time for me to fall in love, to get married. I am ready to fall in love now.' Her eyes flicker down the busy street. I find myself wondering what her mother would like me to do now. Follow her, I suppose. Eat supper.

She leads me through a *soi* (narrow passage) filled with the scent of oils strong enough to make my eyes smart, towards the mayhem of Khao San Road, lined with bars and thumping music, with shops selling clothes of every hue, with enticements to a massage, with restaurants spilling punters onto the pavements. Stalls sell a jumble of fabrics, wooden animals, second-hand books, jewellery; street food fills the air with the smell of frying. Everyone seems to be smiling. Anke gorges on a spring roll; I am not hungry – well, only for more of this delightful depravity. Bangkok has a seedy reputation, but – at first glance – there seems no doubt that people are enjoying the debauchery.

We venture into tiny *soi*, to find more massage parlours, tattoo opportunities, body piercing, hotels with 'day rates', and men in dreadlocks comatose in corners. Anke is, immediately, scathing. 'Bloody fools. Why come here to take drugs? The penalties – prison. For years. Crazy – just go to Holland and do it legally. There's no point in coming all this way just to get stoned.' I wonder what Russell and Tamsin would reply to that.

There is no sign of Anke at breakfast the next morning, but she rushes up to me as I set out, urging me to sit with her while she eats. She has decided to stay one more day, but will definitely leave tomorrow.

'Look at that.' She points to a saggy white man with a young Thai woman on his arm. 'Pathetic. That's what it is. They think they're so clever, with this young thing sucking up to them.' Her venom surprises me.

'What these men don't realise,' she carries on, 'probably because they are too stupid to think that much, is that these girls earn their living this way. They get food, and presents for their families, and they'll make all sorts of promises when they wave him off, a quick email to say sorry, and then off with someone else next week. And the men can't see it – look at him!' She points to a slight man, his grey hair wisped across a peeling bald patch, baggy beige shorts revealing crumpled legs, almost drooling over the woman by his side. 'Can't get it anywhere else; pays for two weeks here and shags himself silly; goes home and cries for a month. Pathetic. Grotesque.'

I love the easy solutions of youth. She spouts opinions; last night it was drugs and today it is seedy old men. But I find myself behaving like a teacher, challenging her. 'I wonder if it's more complicated than that. I mean – who's exploiting who? Okay, so there's nothing attractive about seeing that bloke salivating over her like that; but she gets money; he acts out his fantasies. I mean – she is adult. It would be different if she were younger, but she must be your age at least – twenty,

twenty five?' I'm not sure I believe what I'm saying. Maybe I'm only engaged in this conversation because opportunities to delve into ideas have been so rare.

The man and his floozy wander on. Anke forgets them instantly, and plunges into what she really wants to talk about – her father.

'It is hard,' she says. 'Last time I was here he was alive. Somehow it is harder, with him not here. I mean – not that he was in Thailand with me, that was my boyfriend, my ex-boyfriend; I mean it's different knowing my father is nowhere. I thought it wouldn't be a problem, but I think about him all the time, wonder what he would tell me to do. I hadn't expected it to be like this.'

'It is different for everyone,' I tell her, lamely. 'There aren't any rules for coping when someone dies. You must do what feels right for you now. Besides, surely he would want you to be happy – he would want that more than anything else?'

She agrees; I wonder why I am getting into this conversation. I will not talk about my own grief, nor speculate on the sorrows of my daughters – it feels too personal, too intrusive. Besides, she is too needy to care about anyone else's distress. Our chatting begins to take a counselling shape; it's time to head off, explore the palace, anything rather than absorb Anke's needs. She has to work this out for herself.

I meander off for an idle day. But as I sit with my diary in the late afternoon mayhem, Anke slides beside me again.

'No,' she tells me, 'I've not got anything sorted yet. I might go to Koh Samui tomorrow. I've seen a website, there is some sort of health place there; they offer a colonic experience.' I can't tell her that I think she is looking for something more comforting than a pipe in her bottom. We agree to meet for supper.

'Or I could go home. I've finished my course – but I need to go back to uni.' She is, suddenly, briefly, lively, overtaken by her own intelligence. And then her eyes cloud over; her need for a substitute parent remains unmet.

She is still here the following evening.

'The reason I didn't go today,' she tells me. 'is because there were no rooms in the health place I was looking at; I think I'll go tomorrow. I might go to Koh Chang. It sounds quiet, and maybe there is a health spa there.'

'I'm off to Cambodia tomorrow,' I remind her. 'Will you go to Koh Chang, do you think?'

'I don't know. Maybe I just can't handle this. I thought I could, but, well, there are family things going on at home.'

I wait.

'My brother,' she says, 'it's his birthday, and, well, there's family stuff and maybe I should be at home.' She diverts from her food to ring a friend in Holland, ask him to find out if she can change her flight, to go home in the next day or two. She assures him she has not made up her mind, but just wants the information. For the twentieth time I wonder what her mother would have me do. Send her home, probably.

55.

As I had warned Anke, I am heading for Cambodia. It is the kind of trip that haunted my worst fantasies before I left home. Now, I swing my rucksack onto my back, and step off into the unknown with no more thought than if I were popping into town. (That's not entirely true; I can't do the rucksack-swinging thing. I have to put it on the bed, or in a chair, sit and wriggle backwards into it, and then stand up.)

I have a long trip to the border, beginning with the challenge of insisting that the taxi driver uses his meter. There are no problems with assertion now. Then hour after hour on a bus, through flat industrial Thailand. There are miles of wet: rivers, canals, lakes and ponds. Through working towns, with small supermarkets alongside traditional buildings. Much of the jungle has been cleared, and we pass trucks laden with lychees, durian, a fruit that looks like a small potato and another that is knobbly and unrecognisable.

We reach Trat at around three-fifteen. I climb, stiffly, from the bus, to wait on a bleak, steamy platform for the connection to take me to the border. The air is heavy, leaden, with no hint of restorative breeze. Even the mosquitoes are lazy. I am waved to a row of blue seats, plonk my rucksack on the floor and myself next to it. Immediately a monk in orange robes gets up and moves away. I have, inadvertently, broken a code; monks may not sit next to women. He leans against a pillar and we make a point of not looking at each other.

We wait for an hour, until the children have come out of school, and the women have sold all they can at the market. There are obviously no rules regarding how many people can be crammed into one minibus.

Another hour, and we reach the border. Long before it is my turn to clamber out my luggage has found its way onto a large trolley; five young men crowd round me. I can't tell if they are Cambodian or Thai, but their lack of stature and drawn faces betrays their history of hunger.

'You want taxi or motorbike to Koh Kong?'

'Taxi,' I say, firmly.

'You are alone?'

'Yes, I am alone.'

'Motorbike; you want motorbike.'

'I am old; I want a taxi.'

'You not old; I drive very slowly. You will see.'

Meanwhile my luggage has disappeared and I am herded towards a little office to get my visa. Their attention makes me smile; while their motivation is financial there is no difficulty in exchanging grins. I need persistence to keep control over anything that is going on, but enjoy the tussle.

'How much is the visa?' I ask, knowing that this can change from day to day (and from tourist to tourist).

'Thirteen hundred baht,' says the lad beside me.

'Twelve hundred baht,' says the woman on the desk, simultaneously. We all smile as I pay her. The lad then reaches for the application form, wanting to fill it in for me, but I insist I can manage this bit myself. Still he hovers while my passport is stamped, then leads me to my motorbike driver. He asks for fifty baht for helping with my visa; the luggage carrier asks for another fifty baht for carrying my rucksack about twenty metres. I smile, give them much less, smile again at their bewildered disappointment. Should I have paid them more? I can afford it. But paying over-inflated prices fuels a belief that tourists are stupid and can be fleeced for as much as possible. Besides, I'm not a tourist; I'm a traveller. They wave me off with no apparent ill-feeling, so I can't have got it that wrong.

The motorbike driver has my rucksack perched in front of him; he can, he assures me, see over it. I try not to clutch him round the corners; and he is, as promised, careful over the potholes. The wind blows in my hair; my skirt flaps around the wheels of the motorbike. It is not elegant, and definitely unsafe; but it is fun.

'I am going to college. I learn English, will it help me?' he shouts, his voice just audible above the roar of the engine and whistle of the wind.

'Yes, it will help you. It is good to go to college.' I have no idea if he is telling the truth and anticipate comments on the cost of his studies. Instead he is anxious to organise my onward journey.

'You do not want the boat. The bus, take the bus. There are rivers to cross; you get a ferry across the rivers. Do not tell the hotel, come with me, I will get you a ticket for the bus.'

'No, I know I want to go on the boat; it leaves at eight. It will be much easier than going into the town and catching a bus.' He persists, seems surprised at my intransigence. We arrive at the hotel, and still he lurks in the hope I'll change my mind, shakes his head in disappointment when I buy my boat ticket from the woman in reception. I tip him generously; even then he hovers. I wish him well and turn, firmly, to go to my room.

It is already late, and I am hungry. The menu in the restaurant is in an Eastern script; I rely on pictures to help me choose. Electricity is precious and we are little more than shadows in the dim fluorescent light; night is black around us. The air hums with mosquitoes. I can hear sizzling from the kitchen, am reassured that my food will be freshly cooked. My prawns and rice are served by a child, about nine years old, with a smattering of English. I am the only non-Asian here, but if there is curiosity they are much too polite to show it.

Paying for my food presents a challenge. Cambodia works in three currencies: Thai baht, US dollars, and Cambodian riel. I have no riel, and few baht left. We settle on dollars; they give me the change in riel.

Back in my room I admit to exhaustion. How can I be so tired when all I have done today is sit?

I ease down to breakfast early. There is no alternative to rice; even after eight months my stomach is surprised by spices early in the day. I manage about a third of it. In daylight I can see the small canal, black and putrid with shimmers of oil and a large paper sack caught in reeds, alongside the restaurant. A man rides past on a motorbike, four children in immaculate school uniforms balanced, somehow, behind him.

Motorbike drivers persist in their efforts to give me a lift to the ferry – less than a hundred metres up the road. As I arrive one man grabs my rucksack and swings it on board; I give him a thousand riel, knowing it is puny but I have no other change. Two men harangue me; I am adamant that he has earned no more. There is posturing on both sides and the moment passes.

Meanwhile, the boat is filling with boxes of fruit, labelled with pictures of mangosteen and lychees and durian; these are heaped on the back seats leaving passengers to make the best of the benches at the front. There is the inevitable smell of crushed people, mingled with uncrushed fruit. A trip to the toilet involves scrambling on top of the boxes of fruit, then dropping down to crawl through a little door; the pong suggest that few men compensate for the rocking of the boat.

We sit low in the water and I can see little through the splattered window. My *Lonely Planet* warns that these are riverboats, and not designed for choppy coastal waters. Especially when overladen with fruit, and people, and – as I see through the window at the front – a couple of motorbikes. It occurs to me that the only things that might survive if the boat goes down are the motorbikes. Will they float, I wonder? As if, when the time came and I was sinking amid the lychees and mangosteen I would give a toss about the flotation capacity of a motorbike. A woman next to me practises her few sentences of English; it is not enough to call itself a conversation but we smile to each other from time to time. Her smiles make me feel welcome, as if someone wants me here. The ferry potters southwards, past the occasional island and fishing boat; we stop once and somehow more people find room to sit.

There are crowds to welcome us in Sihanoukville; most are waiting to help with the fruit. I wander along the jetty unmolested. But when I ask for a taxi the fun begins. I haggle my fare down to five dollars, my young driver muttering all the way to his car.

The door safely closed, he smiles. 'Sorry, you want taxi so I must pay off the motorbikes, and I must pay my friend, I have borrowed his car. And I have studies.'

This sounds like the same script I heard yesterday. 'What are you studying?'

'English, at the university. One day I will be a tour guide. I can take you on a tour.' Anything could be true; or not. But his English is reasonable, and he seems comfortable with me asking questions. We negotiate a tour in a few days, agreeing that a motorbike will take us along tracks to beaches and waterfalls I might not otherwise see.

'You come from Sihanoukville?'

'No. My family is from the border with Vietnam; they grow rice; there is nothing else there. I have come here for work.'

'Is it difficult to find work?'

'Everything is hard. Even with education it is hard. The government is corrupt; they control everything. If we cannot pay, then we cannot do it.'

I am waiting for him to wonder how to make it to England, but that does not come.

'And there is no work,' he persists. 'Even here there is no work. Only motorbikes. All we can do is ride motorbikes; and now so many of us, so still no money. We need tourists. Soon we will have international airport; then there will be work.'

Welcome to Cambodia!

56.

I have a dilemma. The weeks are passing and my curiosity is intact. I know I can do this now. There is a world to see, and I want to see it. But my body is telling me to stop for a while. It is an unfamiliar feeling, but – at last – I listen. I splash out on a hotel with a pool, and check in for twelve days. Surely long enough for my body to catch up with the enthusiasm in my head.

I potter by the pool; hours drift. I can't believe I can sit and do nothing for so long. I do not recognise my own lethargy. In conscious moments I try to grapple with the history of Cambodia, précised in the pages of my *Lonely Planet*. The early centuries, when Angkor Wat was built, is painted as a procession of passing dynasties, the ebb and flow of Asian glories. My determination to absorb these details is, I know, simply a postponement of reading about more recent horrors.

This is a story I know; it reached the Western papers, even pricked the conscience of Hollywood. The Khmer Rouge, imbued with the terrifying thinking of Pol Pot, attempted to reshape the population, returning everyone to the land. Education was outlawed; teachers, lawyers, architects – fled or were killed. Millions died. Only a Vietnamese invasion brought an end to the regime, but still the country suffered as political wrangles around the world left Cambodia ravaged by a culture of fear, violence and retribution.

There are elections now, but corruption is an open secret. The country is trying to rebuild, but the architects are dead and there is nobody left who knows how to make bricks.

I don't really want to read about this. I know what one person can do to another – I spent my working life with it. But this is terror on a grand scale, beyond anything imaginable. I am caught between wanting to flop about, soak up the sun like a tourist, and knowing I must read this if I am to spend any time here – if only out of respect to those who survive. The *tuk tuk* drivers who gather at the front of my hotel grew up in terror – not the manufactured terror created in western media, but the reality of genocide on their doorsteps. Mothers slashed and raped. Fathers decapitated, skulls paraded as warnings. Crouching in rank paddy fields, buzzing with mosquitoes, trying to suppress the sighs of breathing while soldiers swept by.

I persist, one paragraph at a time. I don't have to like it; but do have to read it.

I cannot, I decide, sit about all day. I take a sandy track to Serendipity Beach, with its soft white sand and ragged beach shacks. I sense disappointment each time I fail to stop. I can't count the beggars, those with legs blown off by land mines struggling on makeshift crutches, the blind man with his arm on the shoulder of a child, the children with handfuls of beaded jewellery. Pale-skinned tourists in skimpy swimsuits brush them away.

I am intrigued by a sign leading to the Cambodian Children's Painting Project. At first glance there is little to distinguish it from other beach shacks; a small bar in one corner with a collection of chairs and tables beside it. Opposite the bar are several high boards decorated with a collection of small paintings.

Sokha approaches me and explains, 'The children come here; they paint if they want to, and the pictures are sold for four dollars. The children get two dollars, and we keep two. We give them good food at lunchtime. And clean water.' He waves to a plastic drum with a small tap. Children amble around him.

One tugs at my sleeve. 'Where you from? You buy my picture?'

'I am looking at all the pictures,' I try to assure him, knowing pictures would be ruined if they had to live in my rucksack for four months. A small boy crouches by a low table, reaching for a board and a paintbrush. Another meanders in from the beach with a tray of jewellery and flops on a chair. A little girl reaches for Sokha's hand; he glances at her and ruffles her hair.

'I used to work with children who had been hurt, before I came here,' I explain.

'Then you must come tomorrow.' He grins at me, as if I am the one person he wants to come to the party. 'You must come; Bobby is going back to England.' A portly man, sitting by the bar, turns to face us and repeats the invitation.

Slowly I discover the story of the project. One day, when Sokha had no work, he lingered on the beach, distracted by the antics of the children. He watched as they hassled tourists for money, rifled through bags hidden beneath the towels of swimmers, waved glimpses of their pants at lonely men. He talked to Bobby, an English artist, and together they dreamed up the Painting Project: Bobby providing some money and know-how, Sokha devoting himself to the children. They have, slowly, attracted tourists, some of whom sponsor children to attend school.

'I go to the school soon,' Sokha says; 'you will come with

me? See – I have a chart – I show good marks, there is a chart for good marks. I tell the children well done.' I don't need to ask why their parents are unavailable for such tasks.

I am not sure about the party; I don't want to gatecrash. But invitations pour from all quarters and it is clear I will be welcome. And so I put on a clean (well, almost) skirt and return the next day.

A trestle table laden with fruit is in the middle of the children's space; only one small boy steals a mangosteen. Women gather around fires contained in cast-iron frames, cooking small meatballs (for the children); one sits with a tray of prawns in front of her and urges me to buy one. One small girl, sullen and unsmiling, clings to my arm; another warns me not to play with the mangy dogs as they might bite me. A boy comes up with a one-pound coin that he has 'found'; I give him two dollars for it and he beams. I lose count of children clamouring to pose for photographs; I am drowning in children.

This party is not about games; the focus is food. First the meat, and then fruit; somehow Sokha keeps order of an unruly queue and makes sure even the smallest gets her share. Bobby's turn: he throws packets of crisps into the throng; this time Sokha needs to comfort little ones who are trodden on.

Gradually some of the children meander away; a few linger to make a painting; some flop on the arms of my chair, rush off, then rush back again. A grubby boy drops a hanger laden with beaded necklaces in my lap and joins his friends to play football.

Of course I return – day after day. I cannot resist the children. Two days later, I am enjoying a coconut ice when Matt, a lanky English nurse wanders in; he asks if I know where he can buy water. His eyes scan the little pictures and he turns back to me.

'This is wonderful. How are they funded? Do you know?'

'I know the paintings bring in money, and tourists must

give them some.' I've loved every minute of being with the children and given little thought to funding. (It is a trait my daughters recognise.)

'You see,' he goes on, 'I help to run a small trust in England and we are always looking for small projects like this, that have no other money, run by local people. We have worked with an orphanage in India, and are setting up a play project in South Africa at the moment.'

I wait for a pause in the children and wave Sokha over. Matt eases into the money question; Sokha struggles with his English but suddenly he seems to realise the potential of this impromptu meeting and can find no words at all. Matt helps with direct questions: who buys the paints, the boards, do they pay rent? It is clear that Bobby has handled the money.

'We don't know if we can stay here,' Sokha waves into the space around him. 'The owner, he wants more rent, can get more money from a beach shack than from us. More money, I don't know . . .' His voice tails off.

'How much,' Matt is persistent. 'How much is the rent?'

'One thousand dollars, maybe more?'

'For a month?'

'No, for a year.'

Matt and I exchange glances.

'I can't promise anything,' he assures Sokha, 'but I will do my best to get you enough to pay the rent. Then you can stay here. Can you write me a proposal?'

Sokha goes as pale as a Cambodian can go.

'I can write a proposal.' It absorbs all afternoon and evening, but is straightforward. Later I learn that funding – just for one year – is secured.

57.

We gather the next morning, to sip coconut ice and go over the proposal. Sokha is pulled backwards and forwards by the children; it is a pragmatic meeting. But, just as he thinks he has time to read it, Gardner – a lean American nurse with thinning hair – arrives. He comes, we learn, monthly, from Phnom Penh, armed with supplies for the first aid kit. Ratana, a fragile young Khmer woman, hangs on his arm while he pulls out bandages and plasters and bottles of iodine. He turns to a small girl with a graze the length of her forearm, a familiar injury from falling off a motorbike; blood drips down her fingers onto the wooden floor. Gardner offers to show Sokha the correct method of cleaning and dressing the wound.

'This will hurt,' he warns her. I crouch beside her, hold her hand while Gardner pours iodine cross the wound. She is shaking slightly. Silent tears trickle down her cheeks.

And here it all goes cloudy. The world reels. Totters. Goes black. I feel as if a tornado has spun across my head. Through the haze I hear Matt ask, 'Are you epileptic?' He and Gardner are each holding a hand. I am flopped in a chair.

'You've had a seizure.'

That's impossible. I've never had a seizure. Matt mutters soothing rubbish.

Gardner plunders me with questions. 'Did you see anything? Did you smell anything? Squeeze my hand; squeeze Matt's hand; is there any difference? At our age – I'm sixty-one – we must be careful. We can get strokes. I'm not saying you've had a stroke; look at me, smile. You look okay, but still, we can't tell. You must stay in our hotel tonight; you mustn't be alone. Tomorrow we can take you to a doctor in Phnom Penh. Where is your hotel? Your key? We'll move your things.' He asks questions that assume I'm capable of coherent thought, then provides instant answers for me when it's obvious I'm not.

I feel slightly sick; can't organise myself. The afternoon careers around me. It takes hours before I can arrange a sentence to make any sort of sense, and by then my hotel move is organised and bus ticket bought.

I turn to Matt. Gardner has taken over, but I trust Matt. 'Do I really need to do this? Can't I just rest for a few days?'

He looks at me with gentle, worried eyes. 'You must see a doctor. It may be nothing, but you must find out. It isn't safe for you to carry on without being sure it won't happen again.'

Eventually I sit up, reconnect with the beach. Sokha hovers; it seems he has been by my side for most of the afternoon. The little girl, her injury neatly dressed, sidles up beside me. She strokes my arm. Her brown eyes are full of alarm.

'You okay?' she asks. It is the closest I get to tears.

I sleep fitfully, my mind wandering from one false solution to another. Gardner is the first to bang on my door in the morning. He insists that we tell the doctor that I didn't sleep well; he can't hear that not sleeping is a symptom of my situation and nothing more. Matt calls, and then Sokha, their eyes still heavy with unease. I totter down for breakfast; Gardner is out; Ratana and I flounder with a splintered conversation. What is there to talk about with a beautiful, fine-boned Khmer woman of twenty-four who is captive to an American aged sixty-one? If I had the energy I might try to mother her.

I head upstairs to pack. I am light-headed, feel as if thoughts are floating in the mind-ether somewhere and I can't quite grasp them. Hurrying is impossible.

Gardner appears after half an hour; my sluggishness worries him and he takes my pulse, shines a torch in my eyes, repeats checks for one-sided weakness. He is flushed with excitement; I find even anxiety elusive. It is a strange state, being central to a drama that doesn't feel a proper part of me.

It is two hundred and forty kilometres to Phnom Penh.

Four hours on a rickety bus beside miles of muddy rice paddies, shacks on wonky stilts, rubbish heaped in trenches by the roadside; through the occasional town, with milling people and animals; great stretches of water with a stink that I cannot name: it even seeps into the bus's air conditioning.

But my mind is shrinking.

I almost wonder how much more of such destitution I can bear to see. Would I not be better, safer, healthier, in the green fields of Wiltshire? Wearing clothes that are really clean, with doctors down the road, and jacket potatoes and cheese? And daughters.

Suddenly, as we drive into the city, the glorious roof of a wat is etched against the polluted skyline. Even daughter fantasies dissolve and I know, again, why I am here. I am a traveller now.

I can't bear it if the journey has to end here.

58.

We climb the steps to reach Gardner's flat, stumble into a small kitchen with toilet and shower partitioned off it. Beyond is a narrow corridor, with two bedrooms to one side and, at the far end, a sitting room crammed with books, videos, and teaching materials. Even with fans on full, the flat is stifling.

For all my determination, I am struggling. I sit for a while, unravel my luggage, sit again. There is no coherence in my thinking, and little in my actions. Everything has to be done slowly. I don't recognise myself.

I must sleep. There is a catfight in the dawn hours. Somewhere a child screams, a high screech that echoes, and suddenly stops. Tomorrow I will see a doctor. If a Khmer woman has a fit, what happens to her? I know the answer, but it does not sit easily.

Gardner preaches to Ratana over breakfast. She is, apparently, curious about why I am travelling. He tries to explain the curiosity that can come with affluence, but it remains a mystery to her; she gives up and returns to bed.

He turns to me. 'I am trying to teach her. There are so many things she needs to know. Terrible things have happened. She has so much to learn. She can't understand that life will be easier for her when she sees things differently.'

I keep my own counsel.

The American Medical Facility is housed in the basement of an extravagant hotel. Gardner tells the story; he has to – I remember nothing. There are questions; I seem to be having a problem making myself understood, as if the woolliness that still coats my thinking extends into jumbled sentences and mistimed answers. Eventually we agree that I need an assessment but would like to carry on travelling if it is safe to do so. Dr Rick makes no promises; a seizure can be serious, or simply a fleeting event with no future implications.

But we have to wait for my insurance company. The time difference doesn't help. I am instructed to rest, to stay somewhere cool. Gardner and I sit by the muddy waters of the Mekong. It is a black, sluggish river; while I can see no dead dogs it reminds me of the brackish Ganges at Varanasi. But the sun does not give prizes for cleanliness; the water sparkles; fishing boats bob romantically by (although I know there is nothing romantic about their arduous labours). I don't want to go home.

It is late afternoon before we learn that the insurance company is trying to insist I fly straight to London. Dr Rick argues for an assessment in Bangkok, and the decision remains in the air. It is, however, clear that I will not be leaving today.

I sit under the blast of air conditioning in Gardner's flat, and imagine Anna, my eldest daughter, getting a call from a nameless insurance bureaucrat to tell her I am ill and coming home. I must tell her first.

And I have to do it quickly, before I can bear to think.

'I'm fine – there's really no need to worry. It's all very silly, a storm in a teacup, I'll be right as rain in a day or so.'

'So what has happened?'

'Well (deep breath) I had a seizure, so I really need to get it checked out. But there are no facilities here, so it looks like I'm heading for Bangkok – unless they make me go home. I just thought I should let you know. I'm sure it will all be sorted in a day or so.' And she is gone.

I can't believe I have done this to her.

After all the encouragement they have given me – the funny texts and emails, the enthusiastic comments on my blog – and now this. Whatever worries they may share behind my back they have never nagged me. Never mentioned the alarms that my parents raised when I muttered about travelling, all those years ago. Never even voiced any of the qualms I dared to consider for myself. Instead they threw me a party, to wish me well. They were proud of me. I couldn't have done this without them.

That phone call is the most heart-stopping moment of my trip. I send a text: there really is nothing to worry about. The reply: it's not your decision whether we worry or not. Her words are crisp, brittle. I send emails; I try to insist that I am fine. I have no way to make them believe me. I want to behave like a mother, make the world all right for them.

I cannot escape from Gardner and Ratana.

'Show Jo your photographs,' he commands. She is clearly reluctant at first, but brings out an album full of pictures of herself.

'She does some modelling, and some film work. She doesn't get paid, of course. Look – that's where you were fat, remember Ratana? You look better here, when you are thin.' I swallow my objections; she will, apparently, be in another film in a few days. I dare not ask.

We go to Lakeside for supper. Men line the roadside offering drugs, miming smoking or a quick snort. There are cheap rooms and ill-lit bars; Ratana greets friends at every turn. But the restaurant, perched above the lapping of the lake, is clean and well-enough lit. The water barely smells.

Gardner fiddles with his phone.

'What are you trying to do with it?' Ratana asks.

'It has broken; I want to turn off the volume, but it has broken and I cannot do it.'

'Give it to me. I know how.'

'It's broken; it's not about not knowing how. Bloody thing.' Ratana is, initially, amused, convinced she can solve the phone problem. He is equally convinced that it is broken and won't give it to her. Stalemate; Ratana refuses to speak to him.

He scrapes his chair back. 'I've had enough of this.' And he is gone.

She looks at me for a minute, then thinks she had better go to look for him. I gaze across the lake, eat my supper, feeling like the mother of adolescents waiting for them to return home after a hissy fit. It takes ten minutes for Gardner to come back.

'Where is she?'

'She went to look for you.'

'I went to the toilet; I said that's where I was going. This is what she does, you see; the minute she can't cope with something she just runs off. Time and time again. I even went to a counselling place. They said she feels unsafe, because of all the things that have happened to her. Each time she threatens to leave I should buy her something; eventually she will learn that she is safe with me. Already I have bought her a wardrobe and an ironing board.'

We finish our meal and drift through back streets looking for her. No one has seen her. Back at the flat, Gardner reaches for the phone; I go to bed.

I can't stay here. I want no part of their drama. Ratana is young, beautiful and manipulative; Gardner is old, patronising and a bully. In the morning, having established that Ratana is safely home, I tell Gardner that I can see that he and Ratana need time to themselves and I am in the way, that I will look for a hotel with a pool. If I must go home, then at least I'll go out in style. His protest is feeble; he promises to help me move, then returns to their room, sending Ratana out to speak to me.

'I am sorry; I know I shouldn't go off like that. I shouldn't tell lies that I am looking for Gardner. Please stay; I know it is my fault you want to go. Please stay.' I try, pathetically, to maintain that they need time alone together. I want to hug her, to whisper in her ear and tell her she should leave him. But Gardner hovers over both of us.

The Cambodiana Hotel, with the medical facility in its basement, is expensive, and my room with magnolia walls and potted palm could be anywhere in the world, but I don't care. Gardner brings my luggage, and we sit in the elegant café with coffee.

'I was going to marry Ratana, but after last night, well I'm not sure. She must stop running off like that. I'm not sure how long I can cope with that.'

'Maybe thinking again is a good plan.'

He is leering at a young waitress and seems not to hear me. 'Asian women are so beautiful; I think I am already in love with her. I don't know why, I'm just not interested in American women, but the women here – there is something about them. Even better than Thai women.' He is referring only to women under twenty-five.

If I weren't feeling ill I might have the energy to despise him.

Meanwhile Dr Rick succeeds in arranging my transfer to Bangkok. He rings me, his deep brown voice full of reassurance. I sink into a soft pillow and sleep.

59.

I feel as if my stomach is trying to eat itself. I force down breakfast. I share the lift to the basement – where Dr Rick has his office – with a maid and twenty trays of cakes. Even a mountain of strawberries and chocolate cannot comfort me.

Dr Steve, who accompanies me to the airport, is given instructions that I must be mollycoddled. I check in, and am passed to Dr Nisa, a short, tubby woman in a blue top with DOCTOR blazoned across her bosom, who bustles from her incoming flight to greet me. Dr Steve gives a history; 'grand mal,' he tells her, with dates and details and my, apparently worrying, presentation when I first arrived in Phnom Penh. She asks for my version of events; I still find it difficult to organise my thinking and present a wobbly story. She nods anyway. She shuffles me to the plane.

Two white-coated young people rush towards me as I wander from the baggage hall in the enormity of Bangkok airport; one takes my arm, leads me out of the building. I feel as if I am in a strange film. There is a blast of Bangkok heat and then the singing of an ambulance, and me – pressed onto a stretcher in the back with blood pressure monitor on one arm and a heart machine bleeping. All I can see through the high back windows are sky and treetops and the underside of an expressway.

The hospital absorbs me. A nurse sinks a cannula into the back of my hand, blood is taken, saline injected. Forms to fill in; questions to answer. She gives me regulation beige pyjamas; they feel like a uniform and I am dressed in compliance. My blood pressure is checked and checked again. An EKG, with little sucky cups leaving circles across my chest. Dr Piboon, a moonfaced man, introduces himself as the representative of the insurance company. He asks for my story (again), asks me how to spell 'beach' and does not understand when I try to explain my woolly-thinking.

'And your family? Your family are not with you?' He frowns in disbelief when I try to explain the joys of solitary travel. 'They must be worried. It is not good for you to be alone.'

This is not the time, nor the place, to have this discussion. I know now how much I love travelling alone, and that my family will be worried, and that the two are not incompatible.

He insists on a second EKG; there is a flurry of nurses and paper spews on and on.

'Have you had heart problems before?' The question is absurd; I assume there is a translation problem. But I am rushed off for an ultrasound.

'The EKG lied,' Dr Piboon announces: 'your heart is fine. You are hungry?' Breakfast was six hours ago.

'The patient is hungry.' I am wheeled along corridors, into a lift, along more corridors and into room 1541. It is a sterile room, dominated by its hospital bed, with small fridge and microwave, a boiler for water and a set of plates. My tuna salad arrives just as the porter reappears with a wheelchair; I shovel food down my throat. Then off for an EEG, with my hair stiff with gel and two nurses chatting across me with occasional nudges in an effort to keep me awake. Back in the wheelchair, I am parked in a corner like a potted plant. A second ultrasound, on my carotid artery: here Dr Chan introduces herself and asks about my journey.

'This is fine,' she tells me: 'just the occasional a-rhythm, but that's what we get at our age.' There is the joy of middle-aged recognition before I am whisked away – and then abandoned again. The corridor is curved; everything, it seems, is just round the corner. I inhale – looking for the smell of cabbage or disinfectant – anything that would confirm my presence in a hospital. But find only the faintest whiff of floor polish.

Nurses rush by. I seem to be the only person in regulation pyjamas. Without warning a porter appears from nowhere, grabs the wheelchair and, without explanation, wheels me back to my room. A nurse marches in, plonks down a tray of food; but I'm not hungry. I sink into a chair on my balcony, the sweaty pollution of the city thick around me; I find no reassurance in car-hoots from the streets far below.

Just as I decide I have been abandoned for the night another porter appears, with another wheelchair: time for the MRI. My head and neck are braced and I am manoeuvred into the machine, drowned in thuds and squeaks and whistles for an hour; at last it is over. Again I am plonked in a corridor; this time I can see a television screen, the hospital 'infotainment' intended, I presume, to distract me from my own exhaustion. The clock clicks round to 7.50 pm.

I am, at last, returned to the relief of my room.

'Nothing more tonight?' Nurses confer – no, nothing more tonight. They check my blood pressure and temperature one last time, give me two pills.

'What are these for?'

'For sleeping.' I swallow them, obediently. I shower, finding brief relief in cleaning the EEG goo from my hair. It is the only thing I have done all day that is my choice. I have fallen into hospital helplessness, and cannot muster the resources to combat it. I almost have the energy to make tea but know I will not stay awake long enough to drink it.

I wake and sleep; wake and sleep. I drag myself into consciousness when breakfast arrives, drop off over my coffee. I am given another pill, for my thrombosis, I am told. As if I know what thrombosis she is talking about. Two small women in sky-blue shirts come in to empty bins, bow, and retreat. A thousand questions should be lining up to frighten me, but I can only doze.

Dr Theeraporn Thaichinda appears.

'I am the neurologist. You know the results of your tests?

I have no idea.

'All is normal; the blood, the heart, the EEG all normal. But the MRI,' he gives a small sigh, 'there is a tiny lesion, a multiple lacunar infarction – it is a tiny cluster of dead brain cells, but so tiny, it is nothing.'

'Why?'

'At our age . .' He does not complete his sentence.

'But,' he resumes, 'it will not happen again. It is nothing to worry about, it is so tiny. It is just one of those things.'

'So I can travel?'

'Yes, you can travel. First you must rest; you can leave here today, tomorrow, and you need to go to hotel and rest for a few days; then you can travel. And each time you travel, you must rest for a day or two. But today, I want you to sleep. And,' he adds an afterthought, 'the insurance company. We see what they say.' I shake his hand.

But my euphoria is short-lived.

Dr Piboon arrives. 'You have seen the doctor?'

'Yes. He says I can carry on.'

There is a sigh. 'But you must rest.'

'Yes, and then . .' I watch as he gathers his English.

'You must stay in Thailand, where there are doctors. Not back to Cambodia. Not on your own. And you cannot drink beer or whisky (I promise not to drink whisky), and no TV, or computer ... '

'No computer – but I need to send emails home.'

'Well, no more than half an hour, and no TV. And you cannot carry a heavy bag. And you cannot walk in the hot days.'

I can see where this is heading. 'You don't agree that I should travel?'

'I think it is not safe for you. You cannot be in the hot days with a heavy bag; and not to Cambodia. It is not safe for you in Cambodia.'

I cannot tell if his reluctance is medical or a prejudice against travelling women, and the words that might muster such a discussion will not arrange themselves. And, without organised words, I have no explanations, no arguments, no ideas. He looks down at me, face full of paternal concern. I feel choices disintegrating. One of us must say the words.

'You think I should go home?' His shoulders drop with relief.

'I think it is best for you and your family if you go home. They will worry. And you need to see doctors in London, to make you better. Then maybe come back.' I long to resist him, to return to the gentle poolside at my guesthouse in

Sihanoukville, to play with the children on the beach. But a corner of me wonders if he is right. This is not just about me. My family are worried. This decision is not mine alone. I have promised I will not take unnecessary risks. I agree to go home.

I take a photograph of my rucksack leaning against the hospital bed. There is no tinsel left.

60.

Two days later, and still there is no flight home. Dr Piboon insists I am well enough to fly alone; the insurance company want an escort and discuss the need for oxygen. As I lie back in my bed I dream of going back to Cambodia, retracing my steps to the bus station, bouncing my way to the border and back to the beaches of Sihanoukville. But as soon as I move around I know it is beyond me; the act of making tea leaves me weary; I run out of tea bags and have to summon the courage to peer out of my bedroom door to find a nurse and ask for more.

I try to find solace in television. BBC World; it feels a planet away. Then, out of the blue, a woman from the insurance company rings. 'The flights, all full. You like to go to a hotel? Or stay in the hospital?' That decision is simple. But it is ten at night when the taxi finally collects me, drives through dark streets where I recognise nothing, and abandons me at a luxurious hotel.

I have no idea where I am. I have no idea if anyone else knows where I am. But at least I am among people. I am lost, but I am free.

I send emails, summon assistance from my brother. He makes phone calls and supervises the machinery that is to organise my return home. Meanwhile I am reduced to the micro-world of the hotel. I drift from my room to the pool to the restaurant. Time loses its shape and days lose their distinction. I read newspapers but retain nothing. I try crosswords, believing that if some brain cells are wobbling I need to keep the survivors in working order, but put them aside after a couple of clues. I lose count of text messages sent and received; my phone is low on money and I agonise trying to decide if I should put twenty or thirty pounds on it; when did such decisions become so difficult?

I miss curiosity. The streets tempt me. I can see the curled roof of a wat from my balcony. Five days ago I would have set off, knowing I might get lost, and that something interesting might turn up in the losing. Now – the thought of being lost is too alarming. It might be an adventure, I try to tell myself. But, for now, I've had it with adventures. I can make it across the road to the internet café, but, when a man staggers drunkenly in front of me, I can't muster a reaction. I am, I realise, not safe in the streets now I can't read them, can't rely on looking out for myself. I stay in the sanctuary of the hotel until, at last, the call comes to tell me a flight is arranged.

I have been away for eight and a half months; and I am on my way home. Dr Pongsak (he tells me to call him Pong) will accompany me home. He is a young man, with fresh-skin and gentle hands; he laughs easily. I am given something to sign, scribble my name without reading it. We are off.

He steers me through the chaos of the airport, patient while I buy presents. I had hoped to buy gorgeous silk for my daughters in Vietnam; these orchids can never be enough, given what I am putting them through. Pong buys chocolate; the women in his office expect chocolate. His job, he explains, is to take sick people home. He understands travelling; more – he understands solitary travelling. We talk of the joy of freedom to make one's own decisions, to linger on mountaintops with no need to reassure anyone by hurrying home.

He settles beside me in the extravagant seats in business class, makes careful medical checks from time to time, ensures I have plenty of water, allows one glass of wine. He is discreetly attentive, and I am grateful. I feel like a woman who matters, not a patient.

The pilot reminds us that it is sixty-four degrees in London; he shivers and reaches for his jacket. A taxi waits for us. We are soon away from the traffic of Heathrow and into the rolling green of England, the reassurance of ripening fields. There is a refreshing smell of rain. We draw up outside my brother's house. His arms enfold me. I spend that night in my niece's bedroom, with its posters of Andre Agassi and a large Siberian tiger. The next day, and daughters have gathered. Not the homecoming any of us would have chosen.

Summer slips away. This, as I have said before, is not a book about being ill, and I don't propose to linger on the details of my recovery. Doctors agree: this is not epilepsy. I have more tests; my heart is fine. My cholesterol is almost fine. But I have antibodies to glandular fever. Did I have glandular fever when I was young? No. I think back to the sore throat on Pulau Tioman, and the sluggish days that followed; the warning of my masseur in the Cameron Highlands. Glandular fever cannot be diagnosed with any certainty, but it makes sense.

The medication I was given in Bangkok eats my thinking. It must be changed. But gradually – for three weeks I take two sets of pills and have no idea where I am or what I am doing. Three months later they are changed again, though the transition is less challenging this time. Slowly, imperceptibly, foggy thinking clears; energy is restored. I seem to have mislaid months. It is over a year before I am, finally, well.

These are reflective months. It takes time to get to know myself again: I am different from the innocent who set sail. At times I still feel battered by the brickbats of my journey. But maybe that is the point; enquiry and the lack of answers is an end in itself; curiosity is exciting and fun and risky and does not need to stop when doors close or years go by.

I write that and immediately there are contradictions. I am –

and I write this tentatively because this is a precious feeling and must not be mislaid – contented. I have been shamed by the misery of destitution and know that I have everything I need. I have touched opulence and know that I have everything I need. I have the luxury of friends and family who love me.

And I am contented with my years. I do not envy the vigour, the enthusiasms, the drives of the young. Indeed, the rhythms of aging suit me; I pause, think, and write because I can no longer rush headlong from one excitement to another. As energy wanes, reflection takes over, allows time to notice the micro-moments that keep us vibrant. The young, I know, do not envy me. They are unlikely to agree that my gap year might have been wasted on them. Indeed, the concept may even seem crazy. But it was the right year for me.

PART TEN

TWO YEARS LATER

61.

I have checked into the same hotel in Sihanoukville. The rooms are as comfortable, the pool as inviting, as I recall. I spend two days relaxing, recovering from jetlag, remembering the heat. I am kinder to myself these days.

But I need to find Sokha. My online enquiries confirm that he has left the painting project, and is now running Sareka House, a project for children who live on the dumpsite, enabling them to go to school. However, he still has a little shack selling paintings on the beach.

I know the way to the beach. I can't quite believe how familiar it all feels. Although the town has grown – this is Cambodia's Blackpool now – the beach shacks are as tumbledown as ever, the beggars as thin.

But the beach itself has changed. The high tide is much higher – high enough to lap the sandbags stacked along the edge of the shacks at one end, where the painting project used to be. I try clambering from one sandbag to another, as the young and lithe do, but my stiff knees rebel and I give up, retrace my steps, take the inland route to the far end of the beach.

Still, my route is blocked. I have no choice but to return to the hotel, try to figure out a plan B. On my way I pass a ragged stall, firmly padlocked, with a board outside: The

Cambodian Children's Painting Project. A hundred yards from where it used to be, and on an inland track, but it's a start. I peer through the grill on the door, scan shelves piled with paints and tiny boards.

It's tidier than it used to be.

A woman emerges from the café next door. 'They are closed. Four days.' I have no idea if the four days begins today, or three days ago, and she doesn't understand my question. I have planned to return to Phnom Penh in three days, then head north to Battambang and Siem Reap.

'Sareka House?' I ask. She looks at me without even raising her eyebrows. Maybe I am pronouncing it wrong. I try again; this time she shrugs.

There is nothing more I can do now but sit in her little café for a drink. And then drag my feet back to the hotel.

I knew finding Sokha would be a challenge, and can't give up yet. I have lost nothing by asking the young women on reception. I show them details, culled from the internet, including an address. They look at each other, chatter in Khmer, and agree they have no idea where it is. But do I have a phone number?

Back to the computer, and I find a phone number; give it to them. I bite my nails while they press buttons, natter into the phone.

'He will be here in half an hour.'

Half an hour. How could it be that easy? One phone call and Sokha is on his way. My stomach does somersaults. Suddenly I don't know what to say to him. How arrogant to think he'll remember me, after all this time. He is a busy man; this is a wasted journey for him. He has obviously spent his two years more fruitfully than I have. He has a new project, more children to care for. I want to see him. I don't want to see him. What sort of hare-brained idea was it to come back here anyway? I am almost counting the minutes.

Which is how I know it is less than half an hour when a motorbike roars up in front of the hotel and Sokha climbs off the back of it. I walk towards him, remembering his frightened eyes, his loose limbs. I recognise his energy. He looks at me, frowning.

'Two years ago,' I begin. And then he smiles, a huge smile. As if I am the one person he wants to see at this moment. Now I know what I need to say to him.

'I came back to say thank you.'

ACKNOWLEDGEMENTS

It must be obvious to everyone that this journey would have been impossible without the support of family and friends at home. Among those who kept the show on the road, I owe a huge debt of gratitude, firstly, to my wonderful daughters: Anna, Tessa, Annie and Polly. Whatever they may have said to each other, their support for me and my travelling was unstinting. They are my unsung heroines. I am also indebeted to both my brothers, and to Pauline Lively, Carolyn Caldwell, Inga Britta Currie, and Lucy Grafen. Between them they made sure I had a home to come back to.

Along the way, I must thank those who joined me, gave me sanctuary, or otherwise made the journey significantly more fun that it might otherwise have been: Bruce and Helen in Australia, Cath Grafen and her poetry in New Zealand, Tika and Shobha in Nepal, Pip Symonds who brought birthday presents half way round the world, Vedesh and his extended family who provided a backstop in India.

And then, of course, there are those who have helped with the book. Firstly I must thank Paul Dodgson, who, as my mentor at Exeter University, encouraged me to transform this book from a somewhat tedious travelogue into something far more entertaining. Thanks, too, to those who have read drafts along the way: Anna Smart (twice – what a star), Carolyn Caldwell, Charlotte Otter, and Gwen Stuart. And to Elaine Connolly, who was recommended by The Literary Consultancy, and did a final copy edit. (I have tweaked it since then – any residual mistakes are mine.)

Finally, a huge thanks to Mark Smart, for his wonderful cover.

7967238R00134

Printed in Great Britain
by Amazon.co.uk, Ltd.,
Marston Gate.